Low Carb High Fat
Top Fat Burning Desserts

©Will Kenton

Forward

"One of the secrets of a happy life is continuous small treats"
- Iris Murdoch

When we think of treats on a diet I am sure we are all thinking sweets, however this is usually a staple that is highly avoided when on a diet. Each of us has some treat we enjoy. Whether it be cookies, cakes or ice creams, I am sure being on the Low Carb High Fat Diet (LCHF) you wouldn't expect to have a whole lot of options for sweet treats. Desserts are one of those things that just make you wonder if your diet is really worth missing out all the little pleasures that life has to offer. We often see sweet treats as obstacles that we tend to steer clear of once we are on a diet. However if you are like me; I am sure that the temptation to have a sweet treat is more than vivid in your thoughts no matter how hard you try to stay away from 'unhealthy' foods. I don't think anyone can resist a sweet treat but we often end up feeling bad after we have indulged.

You are about to be the happiest you could ever be. Desserts are here to stay with you on the LCHF diet and you won't need to feel guilty when you enjoy them. You can still have cakes, ice cream and best of all you can make them all yourself. That's right, you can have "sweet" treats on your LCHF journey, provided that this from this book!

In this book, we share with you a variety of mouthwatering, LCHF sweet treats that can be put together quickly and easily! These recipes are sure to satisfy your sweet tooth.

Whether you're new to the LCHF diet and wondering what type of foods to eat, or a LCHF diet veteran who needs some inspiration, this book is here to inspire!

As you embark on this health journey, I hope it leads you to a life of pure healthy bliss and vitality.

I hope you enjoy this book and the decadent recipes herein, as it was definitely one of my favorite projects to work on.

Bon appetite!

Table of Contents

Forward...3

Dessert Recipes..13
    Chocolate Roll Cake 14
    Caramel Chocolate Brownies..15
    Vanilla & Lime Cheesecake..16
    English Toffee Balls 17
    Fresh Choc-Mint Top Deck 18
    Chocolate & Almond Biscotti...19
    Almond Butter Chocolate Tarts..20
    Strawberry Shortcake 21
    Lemon Soufflés with Poppy seed 22
    Mocha Ice cream 23
    Pumpkin Spice Blondie's 24
    Peanut-Butter Cookie Balls 25
    Honeydew & Vanilla Bombs...26
    Strawberry Ice cream..27
    Coconut Cashew Bars...28
    Pistachio-Almond Bombs..29
    Creamy Avocado Chocolate Ice cream................................30
    Almond Butter Fudge 31
    Blackberry Coconut Porridge..32
    Blueberry Almond Squares...33
    Choc Coffee Bombs 34
    Delicious Creamy Brownies..35
    Macadamia Butter Fudge 36

Lemon Vanilla Cubes	37
Minty Choc Fudge	38
Pumpkin Pie Cups	39
Coconut Cream with Berries	40
Salted Chocolate Macadamia Balls	41
Blackberry Pudding	42
Chunky Chocolate Cookies	43
Blueberry Lime Cake	44
Lime Avocado Sorbet infused with Cilantro	45
Choco-cherry Donuts	46
Maple Pecan Bacon covered in Chocolate	47
Almond Butter and Chocolate Mug Cake	48
Vanilla Latte Cookie	49
Almond Butter and Chia Seeds Bars	50
Lemon Sponge Cake	51
Coffee Cake	52
Chocolate Dipped Macaroons	53
Spiced Lemon Glazed Fritters	54
Cinnamon Bun Balls	55
Raspberry Cheesecake Cups	56
Chocolate filled Fried Cookie Dough	57
Coconut and Macadamia Custard	58
Choco- Almond Butter Ice cream	59
Jelly cookies	60
Almond Butter Truffles	61
Lava Cake	62
Creamy Pistachio Strawberry Popsicles	63
Lemony Cheesecake Mousse	64

Macchiato Cheesecake	65
Lemon and Blackberry Mini Tarts	66
Lemon Soufflés	67
Caramel Pots	68
Whisky Vanilla Mug Cake	69
Maple Pecan Muffins	70
Chocolate Blackberry Panna Cotta	71
Snicker doodle Cookies	72
Chocolate Almond Cookies	73
Lemon & Coconut Balls	74
Chocolate Chia Cream	75
Almond Butter Delights	76
Creamy Lemon Bombs	77
Cream Cheese Balls	78
Gingery Bomb	79
Almond Butter Fudge	80
Spicy Chocolate Bombs	81
Vanilla Muffin Bombs	82
Fresh Basil Coco Balls	83
Choc Chip Almond Butter Cups	84
Almond Vanilla Ice-cream	85
Chocolate Almond Butter	86
Spicy Coconut Balls	87
Coconut Truffles	88
Coconut Dream Bonbons	89
Choc - Fraise Strawberry Treats	90
Decadent Lime Squares	91
Coconut Melon Squares	92

Dark Chocolate Cups	93
Pure Coconut Squares	94
Soft Raspberry Bombs	95
Vanilla Coconut Cakes	96
Soft & Creamy Orange Squares	97
Strawberry Walnut Bombs	98
Watermelon Soup	99
Delicious Nuts Bars	100
Sticky Chocolate Fudge Squares	101
Coco - Raspberry Delights	102
Blueberry Power	103
Chia and Pecan Butter Blondie's	104
Neapolitan Bombs	105
Creamy Orange Bites	106
Pecan Almond Shortbread Cookies	107
Butter Pecan Sandwiches	108
Lemon Meringue Tarts	109
Coconut Ginger Squares	111
Spiced Pumpkin Crème Brulee	112
Almond Butter Bombs	113
Hazelnut Morsels	114
Choco Mint Hazelnut Sticks	115
Chocolate Cookies	116
Chocolate Almond Butter Balls	117
Choc-Orange Walnut Muffin	118
Cinnamon Storms	119
Creamy Orange Bites	120
Coco-Nut Bombs	121

Easy Choc Blueberry Squares	122
Lemon Coconut Balls	123
Gingery Coconut Bomb	124
Homemade Almond Butter	125
Almond Cookies Bombs	126
Hazelnut Squares	127
Lime Mini Muffins	128
Lemony Cream Cheese Bombshells	129
Heavenly Lemon Quads with Coconut Cream	130
Macadamia Cacao bites	131
Minty Galettes	132
Almond Butter Cake with Chocolate Sauce	133
Peppermint Coconut Bombs	134
Pistachio Masala Bombs	135
Raspberry Heaven Bombs	136
Simple Coconut Treats	137
Slow Cooker Pecan Nuts	138
Strawberry Cream-cakes	139
Creamy Strawberry Muffins	140
Walnuts Choc Squares	141
Almond Butter Cake with Choco Sauce	142
Butter Pecan Biscuits	143
Choco Almond Bombs	144
Chocolate-Coconut Layered Cups	145
Chocolate-Walnut Bites	147
Cinnamon Bun Bombs	148
Coconut & Matcha Balls	149
Almond Butter Fudge	151

Rich & Creamy Ice Cream	152
Almond Butter Fudge	153
Blackberry Coconut Porridge with Pumpkin Seeds	154
Choc Coffee-Coconut Bombs	155
Delicious Coconut Brownies	156
Macadamia Butter Fudge	157
Mini Lemony Vanilla Cubes	158
Minty Fudge	159
Pumpkin Pie Bombs	160
Simple Coconut Cream with Berries	161
Cacao Dream Bonbons	162
Berry Cacao Bombs	163
Zesty Candies	164
Coco-Melon Squares	165
Dark Love Cups	166
Coco-Loco Bombs	167
Berry Bliss Pieces	168
Vanilla Cacao Cakes	169
Citrus Flare Bombs	170
Strawberry Dream Bombs	171
All-stars Peanut-Butter Cookies	172
Almond Chocolate Brownies	173
Almond Chocolate Cookies	174
Carrot Flowers Muffins	175
Coconut Jelly Cake	176
Cottage Pumpkin Pie Ice Cream	177
Divine Chocolate Biscotti	178
Halloween Pumpkin Ice Cream	179

Hemp and Chia Seeds Cream	180
Homemade Nuts Bars	181
Creamy Avocado Smoothie	182
Caramel Coffee Smoothie	183
Chia Seed Cream	184
Chocolate Brownies	185
Chocolate Pecan Bites	186
Hazelnuts Chocolate Cream	187
Instant Coffee Ice Cream	188
Jam "Eye" Cookies	189
Lemon Coconut Pearls	190
Lime & Vanilla Cheesecake	191
Chocolate Mousse	192
Strawberry Pudding	193
Kiwi Fiend Ice Cream	194
Minty Avocado Lime Sorbet	195
Morning Zephyr Cake	196
Almond Butter Balls	197
Pecan Flax Seed Blondie's	198
Peppermint Chocolate Ice Cream	199
Puff-up Coconut Waffles	200
Raspberry Chocolate Cream	201
Raw Cacao Hazelnut Cookies	202
Sinless Pumpkin Cheesecake Muffins	203
Sour Hazelnuts Biscuits with Arrowroot Tea	204
Tartar Cookies	205
Wild Strawberries Ice Cream	206
Mini Lemon Cheesecakes	207

Chocolate Layered Coconut Cups 208

Pumpkin Pie Chocolate Cups 209

Fudgy Slow Cooker Cake 210

Easy Sticky Chocolate Fudge 211

Strawberry Cheesecake Ice Cream Cups 212

English Toffee Treats 213

Fudgy Almond Butter Squares 214

Peppermint Patties 215

Buttery Pecan Delights 216

Fudge Oh So Chocolate 217

Cinna-Bun Balls 218

Vanilla Mousse Cups 219

Conclusion.. 220

Dessert Recipes

Chocolate Roll Cake

Serves 12

Ingredients
For cake:
Butter (4 tablespoons, melted)
Psyllium husk powder (1/4 cup)
Coconut milk (1/4 cup)
Erythritol (1/4 cup)
Baking powder (1 teaspoon)
Almond flour (1 cup)
Eggs (3)
Cocoa powder (1/4 cup)
Sour cream (1/4 cup)
Vanilla (1 teaspoon)
For Filling:
Butter (8 tablespoons)
Erythritol (1/4 cup)
Vanilla (1 teaspoon)
Cream cheese (8 oz.)
Sour cream (1/4 cup)
Stevia (1/4 teaspoon, liquid)

Directions
1. Set oven to 350F.
2. Put all dry Ingredients for cake into a bowl and add wet Ingredients one at a time and combine.
3. Line a baking sheet with parchment paper or silpat and spread cake mixture onto sheet. Try to flatten dough as much as possible
4. Bake for 12-15 minutes and cool.
5. Combine filling Ingredients until smooth and spread over cake then use spatula to lift cake and roll into a log.
6. Remove excess filling from edges and slice.
7. Serve. You may chill cake before serving or until ready to serve.

Nutrition Facts (per serving)
Calories 274
Net Carbs 2.8g
Fat 25.1g
Protein 5.3g
Fiber 3.9g

Caramel Chocolate Brownies

Serves 8

Ingredients
Almond flour (2 cups)
Erythritol (1/3 cup)
Maple syrup (1/4 cup)
Psyllium husk powder (1 tablespoon)
Baking powder (1 teaspoon)
Cocoa powder (1/2 cup, unsweetened)
Coconut oil (1/4 cup)
Eggs (2)
Salted caramel (2 tablespoons)
Salt (1/2 teaspoon)

Directions
1. Set oven to 350F.
2. Place all wet Ingredients into a bowl and mix together thoroughly.
3. Combine all dry Ingredients together in a large bowl and add liquid mixture to it; mix together.
4. Grease a brownie pan and add brownie batter to pan. Bake for 20 minutes.
5. Cool, take from pan and slice.
6. Serve.

Nutrition Facts (per serving)
Calories 258
Net Carbs 4.5g
Fat 23.7g
Protein 8g
Fiber 5.9g

Vanilla & Lime Cheesecake

Serves 2

Ingredients
1/4 cup cream cheese, softened
2 Tbsp. heavy cream
1 tsp. lime juice
1 egg
1 tsp. pure vanilla extract
2-4 Tbsp. Erythritol or Stevia

Directions
1. In a microwave-safe bowl combine all Ingredients. Place in a microwave and cook on HIGH for 90 seconds.
2. Every 30 seconds stir to combine the Ingredients well.
3. Transfer mixture to a bowl and refrigerate for at least 2 hours.
4. Before serving top with whipped cream or coconut powder.

Nutritional Facts
Calories 140
Net Carbs 1.38g
Fats 13.04g
Protein 4.34g
Fiber 0.02g

English Toffee Balls

Serves: 24

Ingredients
1 cup coconut oil
2 Tbsp. butter
1/2 block cream cheese, softened
3/4 Tbsp. cocoa powder
1/2 cup creamy, natural peanut butter
3 Tbsp. Davinci Gourmet Sugar Free English Toffee Syrup

Directions
1. Combine all Ingredients in a saucepan over medium heat.
2. Stir until everything is smooth, melted, and combined.
3. Pour mixture into small candy molds or mini muffin tins lined with paper liners.
4. Freeze or refrigerate until set and enjoy!
5. Store in an airtight container in the fridge.

Nutritional Facts
Calories 136
Net Carbs 0.3g
Fats 15g
Protein 1.7g
Fiber 0.04g

Fresh Choc-Mint Top Deck

Serves 6

Ingredients
1/2 cup coconut oil melted
2 Tbsp. cocoa powder
1 Tbsp. granulated stevia, or sweetener of choice, to taste
2 Tbsp. mint leaves (fresh, finely chopped)

Directions
1. Mix the melted coconut oil with the finely chopped peppermint leaves and sweetener.
2. Pour half the mixture into silicon cases or ice cube trays. Place in the fridge. This will become the white layer.
3. Add the cocoa powder to the remaining mixture, then pour onto the white layer which has set in the fridge.
4. Keep refrigerated until set completely.

Nutritional Facts
Calories 161
Net Carbs 0.3g
Fats 18,5g
Protein 0.4g
Fiber 0.07g

Chocolate & Almond Biscotti

Serves 8

Ingredients
1 egg
2 cups whole almonds
2 Tbsp. flax seeds
1 cup shredded coconut, unsweetened
1 cup coconut oil
1 cup cacao powder
1/4 cup Xylitol or Stevia sweetener
1 tsp. salt
1 tsp. baking soda

Directions
1. Preheat oven to 350F.
2. In a food process blend the whole almonds with the flax seeds. Add in the rest of Ingredients and mix well.
3. Place the dough on a piece of aluminum foil to shape into 8 biscotti-shaped slices. Bake for 12 minutes.
4. Let cool and serve.

Nutritional Facts
Calories 276,56
Net Carbs 9.19g
Fats 25,44g
Protein 8,24g
Fiber 5.2g

Almond Butter Chocolate Tarts

Serves 8

Ingredients
For Crust:
Flax meal (1/4 cup)
Erythritol (1 tablespoon)
Almond flour (2 tablespoons)
Egg white (1)
For top Layer:
Cocoa powder (4 tablespoons)
Vanilla (1/2 teaspoon)
Heavy cream (2 tablespoons)
Avocado (1)
Erythritol (1/4 cup)
Cinnamon (1/2 teaspoon)
For the bottom layer:
Butter (2 tablespoons)
Almond butter (4 tablespoons)

Directions
1. Set oven to 350°F.
2. Put flax meal, egg white, almond flour and erythritol together in a bowl and combine.
3. Use mixture to form tart crusts in tart pans and bake for 8 minutes until crusts are set.
4. Place all Ingredients for top layer of tart into a processor or blender and blend smoothly.
5. Take crusts from oven and cool. Combine Ingredients for bottom layer in a microwave safe bowl and heat for 1 minute.
6. Mix together and pour into crusts, level and refrigerate for 30 minutes.
7. Top Almond butter layer with chocolate layer and smooth. Return to fridge for 30 minutes or until set. Serve.

Nutrition Facts (per serving)
Calories 305
Net Carbs 3.9g
Fats 26.8g
Protein 9.8g
Fiber 6.6g

Strawberry Shortcake

Serves 5

Ingredients
For puff cakes:
Cream cheese (3 oz.)
Vanilla (1/2 teaspoon)
Eggs (3)
Baking powder (1/4 teaspoon)
Erythritol (2 tablespoons)

For filling:
Heavy cream (1 cup)
Strawberries (10)

Directions
1. Set oven to 300 °F. Use preferred method to separate egg whites from yolks. Beat egg whites until fluffy and put aside until needed.
2. Add vanilla, erythritol, cream cheese and baking powder to egg yolks and beat together until smooth.
3. Add egg whites a little at a time to mixture and fold to combine.
4. Line a baking sheet with parchment paper or silpat and spread mixture evenly.
5. Bake for 25-30 minutes, remove from oven and cool.
6. Top with strawberries and cream, slice and serve.

Nutrition Facts (per serving)
Calories 178
Net Carbs 2.8g
Fats 16.9g
Protein 2.3g
Fiber 0.5g

Lemon Soufflés with Poppy seed

Serves 5

Ingredients
Eggs (2, separated)
Lemon zest (2 teaspoons)
Vanilla (1 teaspoon)
Ricotta (1 cup, whole milk)
Erythritol (1/4 cup)
Lemon juice (`1 tablespoon, freshly squeezed)
Poppy seeds (1 teaspoon)

Directions
1. Set oven to 375 ℉. Use preferred method to separate egg whites from yolks. Beat egg whites until fluffy and put aside until needed. Add 2 tablespoons of erythritol to egg whites and beat until egg whites become stiff.
2. Add the remaining erythritol and ricotta cheese to the egg yolks and beat until creamy.
3. Add lemon juice, poppy seeds and vanilla to egg yolk mixture. Mix together thoroughly and then add to egg whites a little at a time; fold to combine.
4. Grease ramekins and fill each with batter. Shake gently to level soufflés.
5. Bake for 20 minutes until soufflés are set with a little jiggle.
6. Cool and serve.

Nutrition Facts (per serving)
Calories 151
Net Carbs 2.9g
Fats 10.8g
Protein 9g
Fiber 0.1g

Mocha Ice cream

Serves 5

Ingredients
Coconut milk (1 cup)
Erythritol (2 tablespoons)
Cocoa powder (2 tablespoons)
Xanthan gum (1/4 teaspoon)
Heavy cream (1/4 cup)
Stevia (15 drops, liquid)
Instant coffee (1 tablespoon)

Directions
1. Place all Ingredients into a food processor or blender excluding the gum and pulse until thoroughly combined.
2. Add gum a little at a time while processing until mixture thickens.
3. Process in an ice cream machine or freeze overnight and blend before serving.
4. Enjoy.

Nutrition Facts (per serving)
Calories 145
Net Carbs 1.5g
Fats 15g
Protein 1g
Fiber 2.5g

Pumpkin Spice Blondie's

Serves 12

Ingredients
Butter (1/2 cup, softened)
Egg (1)
Cinnamon (1 teaspoon)
Maple extract (1 teaspoon)
Almond flour (1/4 cup)
Pecans (1 oz., chopped)
Erythritol (1/2 cup)
Liquid Stevia (15 drops)
Pumpkin puree (1/2 cup)
Pumpkin pie spice (1/8 teaspoon)
Coconut flour (2 tablespoons)

Directions
1. Set oven to 350°F.
2. Add butter, egg, pumpkin puree and erythritol to a bowl and beat with a hand mixer until smooth.
3. Add coconut flour, stevia, maple extract, almond flour, cinnamon and pumpkin spice to mixture and mix together.
4. Grease brownie pan and pour in batter.
5. Top mixture with pecans and bake for 25 minutes until golden.
6. Take from oven, cool and slice.
7. Serve.

Nutritional Facts
Calories 112
Net Carbs 1.4g
Fats 10.8g
Protein 1.4g
Fiber 1.3g

Peanut-Butter Cookie Balls

Serves 18

Ingredients
2 cups peanut butter
1/4 cup Erythritol
2 eggs
1 1/4 cups coconut flour
2 tsp. baking soda
2 tsp. peanut extract
1/2 tsp. kosher salt

Directions
1. Preheat oven to 345° F.
2. In a bowl beat the peanut butter, coconut flour and Erythritol with an electric mixer (MEDIUM speed) until fluffy.
3. Reduce speed to LOW and add in the eggs, baking soda, vanilla, and salt.
4. With your hands make balls from the batter and place on parchment-lined baking pan. Bake 10 to 15 minutes.
5. When ready, cool slightly and then move from the stove to cool completely.
6. Serve.

Nutritional Facts
Calories 182,5
Net Carbs 1.4g
Fats 14,67g
Protein 7g
Fiber 1.96g

Honeydew & Vanilla Bombs

Ingredients
1 cup coconut butter
1/2 cup fresh or honeydew
1/2 tsp. sweeter to taste
1/2 tsp. vanilla extract
1 Tbsp. lime juice

Directions
1. Place coconut butter, coconut oil and Honeydew in a pot and heat over medium heat until well combined.
2. In a small blender, add Honeydew mix and remaining Ingredients. Process until smooth.
3. Spread out into a small pan lined with parchment paper. Refrigerate until mix has hardened.
4. Remove from container and cut into squares.
5. Serve.

Nutrition Facts (per serving)
Calories 140
Net Carbs 0,6g
Fats 15.4g
Protein 0.2g

Strawberry Ice cream

Serves 6

Ingredients
Erythritol (1/3 cup)
Vanilla (1/2 teaspoon)
Vodka (1 tablespoon)
Heavy cream (1 cup)
Egg yolks (3)
Xanthan gum (1 tablespoon)
Strawberries (1 cup, chopped into chunks)

Directions
1. Add cream to a saucepan and heat then add erythritol and stir until it dissolves. Do not boil mixture.
2. Beat egg yolks until they are twice their size. Add cream a little at a time to eggs while beating until all eggs and cream are combined; add vanilla and beat together.
3. Add xanthan gum and vodka to mixture and combine.
4. Place into a freezer safe container and freeze for 2 hours or more. You may process through an ice cream machine if you prefer.
5. Add strawberries to ice cream and mix together gently. Return to freezer for 6 hours or more.
6. Serve!

Nutrition Facts (per serving)
Calories 178
Net Carbs 2.8g
Fats 16.9g
Protein 2.3g
Fiber 0.5g

Coconut Cashew Bars

Serves 8

Ingredients
Almond flour (1 cup)
Maple syrup (1/4 cup, sugar free)
Salt (to taste)
Coconut (1/4 cup, shredded)
Butter (1/4 cup, melted)
Cinnamon (1 teaspoon)
Cashews (1/2 cup)

Directions
1. Put flour and butter in a bowl and mix together thoroughly.
2. Add coconut, salt, cinnamon and syrup to flour mixture and combine.
3. Add cashews to mixture and thoroughly mix.
4. Use parchment paper to line a baking sheet and add cashew mixture to the sheet and spread evenly.
5. Refrigerate for 2 hours or more.
6. Slice and serve.

Nutrition Facts (per serving)
Calories 189
Net Carbs 4g
Fats 17.6g
Protein 4g
Fiber 2.1g

Pistachio-Almond Bombs

Ingredients
1/2 cup cocoa butter, finely chopped and melted
1 cup all natural, creamy almond butter
1 cup coconut butter
1 cup coconut oil, firm
1/2 cup full Fatcoconut milk, chilled overnight
1/4 cup ghee
1 Tbsp. pure vanilla extract
2 tsp. chai spice
1/4 tsp. pure almond extract
1/4 tsp. sea salt
1/4 cup shelled pistachios, chopped

Directions
1. Line a 9"x9" square baking pan with parchment paper, leaving a little bit hanging on either side for easy unmolding. Set aside.
2. Melt the cocoa butter in a small saucepan set over low heat or in the microwave, stirring often regardless of which option you chose. Reserve.
3. Add all Ingredients, except for the cacao butter and pistachios, into a large mixing bowl. Mix with a hand mixer, starting on low speed and progressively moving to high until all the Ingredients are well combined and the mixture becomes light and airy.
4. Pour the melted cacao butter right into the almond mixture and resume mixing on low speed until it's well incorporated.
5. Spread as evenly as possible into the prepared pan and sprinkle with chopped pistachios.
6. Refrigerate until completely set, at least 4 hours but preferably overnight.
7. Cut into 36 squares and store in an airtight container in the fridge.

Nutrition Facts (per serving)
Calories 176
Net Carbs 0.4g
Fats 18.8g
Protein 1.8g
Fiber 2.1g

Creamy Avocado Chocolate Ice cream

Serves 6

Ingredients
Hass avocados (2)
Heavy cream (1/2 cup)
Vanilla (2 teaspoons)
Stevia (25 drops, liquid)
Coconut milk (1 cup)
Cocoa powder (1/2 cup)
Erythritol (1/2 cup, powdered)
Chocolate squares (6)

Directions
1. Remove peel and pits from avocados and put into a bowl along with vanilla and coconut milk. Using an immersion blender mix until creamy. If you don't have an immersion blender you may blend in a food processor or blender.
2. Put erythritol in a grinder and pulse until fine.
3. Add ground erythritol to avocado mixture along with cocoa powder and stevia. Mix together until thoroughly combined.
4. Chop chocolate, add to mixture and transfer to a freezer safe container. Cover with plastic wrap and freeze for 12 hours or more.
5. Remove from freezer and use an immersion blender to blend smooth or process in an n ice cream maker as directed by the manufacturer.

Nutrition Facts (per serving)
Calories 241
Net Carbs 3.7g
Fat22.7g
Protein 3g
Fiber 7.5g

Almond Butter Fudge

Serves: 12

Ingredients
1 cup almond butter (unsweetened)
1 cup coconut milk
1 cup coconut oil
1 tsp. vanilla extract
Sweetener of your choice to taste

Directions
1. In a bowl, melt the almond butter and coconut oil.
2. Blend all the Ingredients together well.
3. Pour the mixture into a lined baking pan with parchment paper. Refrigerate for several hours to set.
4. Cut into pieces and serve.

Nutrition Facts (per serving)
Carbs: 4,24g
Fiber: 2,15g
Net Carbs: 0,97g
Protein: 4,45g
Fat: 27,4g
Calories: 295

Blackberry Coconut Porridge

Serves: 4

Ingredients
1/4 cup ground flaxseed
1/4 cup coconut flour
1 tsp. pure vanilla extract
1 cup coconut milk
1 tsp. cinnamon
Liquid sweetener of your choice

Toppings:
1 cup blackberries (any type)
2 Tbsp. coconut, shaved
2 Tbsp. pumpkin seeds

Directions
1. In a saucepan heat the coconut milk. Add in coconut flour, cinnamon, flaxseed and whisk. Add in vanilla extract and liquid sweetener of your choice.
2. Cook for 10 minutes stirring constantly. Remove from heat and let rest for two-three minutes,
3. Decorate with fresh blackberries, pumpkin seeds and shaved coconut. Serve.

Nutrition Facts (per serving)
Carbs: 16,15g
Fiber: 2,07g
Net Carbs: 2,51g
Protein: 0,7g
Fat: 14,15g
Calories: 197

Blueberry Almond Squares

Serves: 32

Ingredients
2 cup coconut oil
1 cup almond butter
3/4 cup blueberries
1/2 cup sweetener of your choice
2 tsp. pure vanilla
salt (optional)

Directions
1. In a small saucepan, melt coconut oil.
2. Add all remaining Ingredients to blender, along with coconut oil and blend until smooth.
3. Pour the batter into an baking pan.
4. Store in refrigerator or freezer.

Nutrition Facts (per serving)
Carbs: 0,5g
Fiber: 0,08g
Net Carbs: 0,35g
Protein: 0,09g
Fat: 19,39g
Calories: 170

Choc Coffee Bombs

Serves: 10

Ingredients
3/4 cup coconut butter
2 Tbsp. coconut oil
4 Tbsp. 100% cocoa powder
2 Tbsp. ground coffee
2 Tbsp. coconut flakes, unsweetened
1 tsp. sweetener of your choice, or to taste

Directions
1. In a microwave, melt the coconut butter.
2. Mix in all the Ingredients (except the coconut oil) and mix well with a fork.+
3. Prepare an ice-cube tray.
4. Spoon the mixture into each cup of the ice-cube tray and gently pat them flat with a fork.
5. Freeze for 4-5 hours.
6. Defrost at room temperature for 30 minutes before serving.

Nutrition Facts (per serving)
Carbs: 1,57g
Fiber: 0,81g
Net Carbs: 0,25g
Protein: 0,61g
Fat: 19,87g
Calories: 178

Delicious Creamy Brownies

Serves: 12

Ingredients
3/4 cup organic cocoa
1/2 cup shredded coconut
1/2 cup walnuts, chopped
1/2 cup full Fat canned coconut milk
2 eggs
1/2 cup Sweetener of your choice
1 cup coconut oil, melted
1 tsp. vanilla extract
1 cup almond flour, heaping
1/2 tsp. baking soda

Directions
1. Preheat the oven to 350 degrees.
2. In a bowl, mix together the coconut oil, coconut milk, vanilla, cocoa, eggs and sweetener.
3. In another bowl combine the shredded coconut, almond flour and baking soda.
4. Combine the two bowls together and pour into a square baking dish.
5. Bake for 30 minutes. Once ready, let cool for 15 before serving. Enjoy!

Nutrition Facts (per serving)
Carbs: 8,73g
Fiber: 3,72g
Net Carbs: 2,17g
Protein: 5,29g
Fat: 27,13g
Calories: 278

Macadamia Butter Fudge

Serves: 12

Ingredients
1 cup macadamia butter
1 cup coconut oil
1/4 cup almond milk, unsweetened
1 tsp. vanilla extract
2 tsp. liquid stevia (optional)
a pinch of coarse sea salt

Directions
1. Combine the macadamia butter and coconut oil with the remaining Ingredients into a blender or food processor.
2. Blend until thoroughly combined.
3. Pour into a 9X4 loaf pan that has been lined with parchment paper.
4. Refrigerate about 2 hours. Serve!

Nutrition Facts (per serving)
Carbs: 4,25g
Fiber: 1,29g
Net Carbs: 2,03g
Protein: 5,39g
Fat: 24,4g
Calories: 284

Lemon Vanilla Cubes

Serves: 12

Ingredients
1 cup extra virgin coconut oil, softened
1 cup coconut butter, softened
1/2 vanilla bean seeds
1 lemon, zest and juice

Directions
1. In a bowl, blend and whisk all Ingredients together.
2. Line a loaf pan with parchment paper. Pour the mixture into the pan, refrigerate for approximately 30 minutes or until firm.
3. Cut into cubes before serving. Decorate with lemon zest. (optional)

Nutrition Facts (per serving)
Carbs: 0,35g
Fiber: 0,01g
Net Carbs: 0,13g
Protein: 0,1g
Fat: 16,77g
Calories: 147

Minty Choc Fudge

Serves: 12

Ingredients
1 cup coconut oil
1 cup organic cocoa powder
1 cup full Fat coconut milk
1 cup sweetener of your choice
1 tsp. peppermint extract
1 tsp. almond extract
1 tsp. Celtic sea salt

Directions
1. Place a sheet of parchment or wax paper along the inside of a loaf pan and place in the freezer for at least 15 minutes.
2. In a bowl, place the coconut oil and coconut milk a medium and mix with a hand mixer on HIGH speed for 5-6 minutes.
3. Add in remaining Ingredients and stir on LOW speed until the cocoa is combined. Add the sweetener of your choice to taste.
4. Pour the batter in a prepared loaf pan. Refrigerate for several hours.
5. Before serving, use a sharp knife to cut the fudge into squares.
6. Serve.

Nutrition Facts (per serving)
Carbs: 4,44g
Fiber: 0,59g
Net Carbs: 2,83g
Protein: 0,51g
Fat: 19,45g
Calories: 183

Pumpkin Pie Cups

Serves: 12

Ingredients
1 cup shredded coconut, unsweetened
1 cup coconut oil
3 cup pumpkin puree, unsweetened
1 Tbsp. ground cinnamon
1 1 tsp. ground ginger
1 tsp. pure vanilla extract
25 drops sweetener of your choice, extract
pinch ground cloves
pinch of Himalayan rock salt

Directions
1. Line a baking sheet with two 12-count mini muffin silicon molds.
2. In a your food processor, add shredded coconut, coconut oil, sweetener of your choice and salt. Blend on HIGH speed for 7-8 minutes.
3. Once smooth, remove 1 cup of the coconut mixture, leaving the remaining coconut mix in the food processor bowl. Add remaining Ingredients and process until smooth again.
4. Scoop about 2 teaspoons into each muffin cup. Press down with fingers or the back of a spoon until completely flat. Then, top with reserved white coconut mixture. Transfer baking sheet to the freezer and freeze for 1 hour.

Nutrition Facts (per serving)
Carbs: 2,83g
Fiber: 1,39g
Net Carbs: 0,95g
Protein: 0,42g
Fat: 11,37g
Calories: 109

Coconut Cream with Berries

Serves: 4

Ingredients
1 can (15 oz) full Fat coconut milk, unsweetened
1/2 cup fresh blueberries
dark chocolate shavings

Directions
1. Store the coconut milk in the fridge overnight.
2. Scoop out the thick part of the coconut milk leaving the water behind.
3. In a bowl, whip with a hand mixer for several minutes.
4. Add in blueberries.
5. Top with chocolate shavings.
6. Serve.

Nutrition Facts (per serving)
Carbs: 9,25g
Fiber: 0,94g
Net Carbs: 4,1g
Protein: 1,48g
Fat: 14,93g
Calories: 167

Salted Chocolate Macadamia Balls

Ingredients
3 Tbsp. Macadamia nuts
5 Tbsp. cocoa powder, unsweetened
1/2 cup coconut oil
2 Tbsp. Granulated Stevia (or sweetener to your choice)
coarse sea salt, to taste

Directions
1. In a saucepan melt the coconut oil. Add cocoa powder and the sweetener. Mix and remove from heat.
2. Pour cocoa mixture into silicone molds until wells are 3/4 full.
3. Refrigerate in silicone molds at least 3 hours.
4. Besprinkle macadamia nuts into each well.
5. Return silicone mold to refrigerator until completely hardened.
6. Before serving, remove chocolates from silicone mold and place on a serving dish.
7. Let sit at room temperature until surface begins to glisten.
8. Enjoy!

Nutrition Facts (per serving)
Calories 201
Net Carbs 0.7g
Fat 22g
Protein 1.5g

Blackberry Pudding

Serves 2

Ingredients
Baking powder (1/4 teaspoon)
Coconut oil (2 tablespoons)
Heavy cream (2 tablespoons)
Lemon Zest (from 1 lemon)
Erythritol (2 tablespoons)
Coconut flour (1/4 cup)
Egg yolks (5)
Butter (2 tablespoons)
Lemon juice (2 teaspoons)
Blackberries (1/4 cup)
Stevia (10 drops, liquid)

Directions
1. Set oven to 350 F.
2. Separate egg yolks from whites and put aside until needed.
3. Place dry Ingredients in a bowl and place coconut oil and butter in another bowl.
4. Beat yolks thoroughly then add stevia and erythritol and combine.
5. Sift dry mix into liquid mixture and mix well together.
6. Grease ramekins and fill with batter and add 2 tablespoons blackberries to each pudding and push in batter.
7. Bake for 25 minutes, cool and serve.

Nutrition Facts (per serving)
Calories 477.5
Net Carbs 5.5g
Fat 43.5g
Protein 9g
Fiber 6.5g

Chunky Chocolate Cookies

Makes 16

Ingredients
Whey protein (3 tablespoons, unflavored)
Psyllium husk powder (2 tablespoons)
Vanilla extract (2 teaspoons)
Stevia (10 drops, liquid)
Egg (1)
Almond flour (1 cup)
Coconut flour (2 tablespoons)
Butter (8 tablespoons, room temperature)
Erythritol (1/4 cup)
Baking powder (1/2 teaspoon)
Chocolate (5 squares)

Directions
1. Set oven to 350 F.
2. Combine almond flour, psyllium husk, whey protein, coconut flour and baking powder together in a bowl.
3. Beat softened butter until fluffy then add stevia and erythritol and beat again.
4. Add vanilla and egg to butter mixture and mix thoroughly.
5. Add dry Ingredients to wet and combine.
6. Chop chocolate and add to cookie dough and mix. Roll into a log and slice into 16 cookies.
7. Flatten each cookie and place onto a lined baking sheet.
8. Bake for 15 minutes, cool and serve.

Nutrition Facts (per serving)
Calories 118
Net Carbs 1.6g
Fat10.8g
Protein 2.6g
Fiber 2.8g

Blueberry Lime Cake

Makes 2 (Serves: 10)

Ingredients
Almond flour (1 cup)
Baking powder (1 teaspoon)
Blueberry extracts (2 teaspoons)
Cream cheese (1/4 cup)
Erythritol (1/4 cup)
Lime zest
Coconut flour (2 tablespoons)
Egg whites (5)
Egg yolks (5)
Blueberries (1/4 cup)
Butter (2 tablespoons, salted)
Stevia (1/4 teaspoon, liquid)
Lime juice (from 1 lime)

Directions
1. Set oven to 325 F.
2. Combine all dry Ingredients for cake in a bowl.
3. Beat yolks thoroughly then add stevia, butter, cream cheese, erythritol and blueberry extract. Mix together until smooth.
4. Add zest and lime juice to mixture and combine.
5. Add dry Ingredients to wet mixture and mix thoroughly.
6. Beat egg whites and lime juice until stiff peaks form then add to cake batter. Fold together until combined.
7. Grease cake pans and pour in batter, top with blueberries and bake for 40 minutes.
8. Cool, slice and serve.

Nutrition Facts (per serving)
Calories 145
Net Carbs 3g
Fat12.4g
Protein 6.4g
Fiber 1.9g

Lime Avocado Sorbet infused with Cilantro

Serves: 4

Ingredients
Hass avocados (2)
Lime zest (from 2 limes)
Lime juice (from 2 limes)
Stevia (1/4 teaspoon, liquid)
Erythritol (1/4 cup)
Coconut milk (1 cup)
Cilantro (1/2 cup, chopped)

Directions
1. Remove peel and pits from avocados and slice thinly.
2. Place avocado slices onto a piece of foil and squeeze 1/2 of a lime over avocados.
3. Place avocados into freezer for 3 hours.
4. Add coconut milk, lime zest and erythritol into a saucepan and heat over a medium flame until it comes to boil.
5. Lower heat and allow to reduce a bit (about 25%). Cool and place into a freezer friendly container and freeze until mixture gets thick.
6. Chop cilantro and add remaining lime juice.
7. Place frozen avocado and cilantro to a food processor and pulse until chunky.
8. Add stevia and coconut reduction and pulse until mixture is smooth.

Nutrition Facts (per serving)
Calories 180
Net Carbs 3.5g
Fat16g
Protein 2g
Fiber 7.25g

Choco-cherry Donuts

Serves 8

Ingredients
Almond flour (3/4 cup)
Chocolate (3 tablespoons, chopped)
Baking powder (1 teaspoon)
Coconut oil (2 ½ tablespoons)
Dark chocolate (5 bars, chopped)
Flax meal (1/4 cup)
Vanilla (1 teaspoon)
Eggs (2)
Coconut milk (3 tablespoons)
Berry extract (2 teaspoons) - you may choose your preferred flavor

Directions
1. Combine all dry Ingredients in a large bowl; in another bowl combine all wet Ingredients.
2. Add wet Ingredients to dry and mix together thoroughly.
3. Add chopped dark chocolate to batter and fold.
4. Heat donut maker and grease then pipe batter into molds. If you don't have a donut maker you may use a donut pan and bake donuts for 10 minutes at 300°F.
5. Cook donuts for about 5 minutes until done.
6. Cool and serve.

Nutrition Facts (per serving)
Calories 107
Net Carbs 1.3g
Fats 9.4g
Protein 3.1g
Fiber 4.8g

Maple Pecan Bacon covered in Chocolate

Makes 13

Ingredients
Bacon (13 slices)
Maple extract (1 tablespoon)
Erythritol (2 tablespoons)

For coating:
Pecans (1/4 cup, chopped
Erythritol (2 tablespoons)
Cocoa powder (4 tablespoons, unsweetened)
Stevia (15 drops, liquid)

Directions
1. Set oven to 400 °F.
2. Line a baking sheet with foil and spread bacon on sheet. Coat bacon with maple extract and erythritol all over.
3. Bake for 40 minutes until bacon is crisp and golden.
4. Pour excess bacon grease into a container. Add stevia, cocoa powder and erythritol to grease and stir until combined.
5. Dip bacon slices into mixture and coat with pecans.
6. Cool bacon slices and refrigerate.
7. Serve.

Nutrition Facts (per serving)
Calories 157
Net Carbs 0.4g
Fats 11.7g
Protein 10.5g
Fiber 0.8g

Almond Butter and Chocolate Mug Cake

Serves 1

Ingredients
Egg (1)
Almond flour (2 tablespoons)
Stevia (7 drops)
Vanilla (1/2 teaspoon)
Almond butter (1 tablespoon)
Butter (2 tablespoons)
Erythritol (1 tablespoon)
Baking powder (1/2 teaspoon)
Dark chocolate (1 bar, chopped)

Directions
1. Combine all Ingredients in a mug.
2. Place in microwave for 2 minutes.
3. Take from microwave and cool.
4. Serve. May be topped with cream.

Nutrition Facts (per serving)
Calories 488
Net Carbs 5g
Fats 47g
Protein 13g
Fiber 6g

Vanilla Latte Cookie

Makes 10

Ingredients
Almond flour (1 ½ cups)
Erythritol (1/3 cup)
Instant coffee (1 tablespoon + 1 teaspoon))
Baking soda (1/2 teaspoon)
Cinnamon (1/4 teaspoon)
Butter (1/2 cup, unsalted)
Eggs (2)
Vanilla (1 ½ teaspoons)
Kosher salt (1/2 teaspoon)
Stevia (17 drops)

Directions
1. Set oven to 350 ℉.
2. Combine coffee, salt, cinnamon, almond flour and baking soda in a large mixing bowl.
3. Separate egg yolks from whites in another container.
4. Put butter into a bowl and beat until slightly fluffy then add erythritol and beat until pale. Put in yolks and continue beating until mixture is smooth.
5. Add half of flour mixture to butter and combine then add stevia, vanilla and leftover flour mixture. Combine thoroughly.
6. Beat egg whites until fluffy and stiff peaks start to form. Add to batter and fold.
7. Spoon mixture onto a lined baking sheet and bake for 15 minutes.
8. Cool and serve.

Nutrition Facts (per serving)
Calories 167
Net Carbs 1.4g
Fats 17.1g
Protein 3.9g
Fiber 14g

Almond Butter and Chia Seeds Bars

Makes 14

Ingredients
Coconut oil (1 tablespoon and 1 teaspoon)
Butter (2 tablespoons)
Stevia (1/4 teaspoon, liquid)
Coconut flakes (1/2 cup, shredded and unsweetened)
Coconut cream (1/2 cup)
Almonds (1/2 cup)
Erythritol (4 tablespoons)
Heavy cream (1/4 cup)
Vanilla (1 1/2 teaspoons)
Chia seeds (1/4 cup)
Coconut flour (2 tablespoons)

Directions
1. Place almonds in a processor and grind finely then add 2 tablespoons erythritol and 1 teaspoon of coconut oil. Mix until thoroughly combined.
2. Heat butter in a saucepan until browned and put in remaining erythritol, vanilla, stevia and cream. Stir to combine and heat until mixture starts to bubble. Add almond mixture to pot and mix together.
3. Put chia seeds into a grinder and pulse until fine and combine with coconut flakes in a pan. Heat pan and toast for a couple of minutes.
4. Combine all Ingredients along with cream, coconut flour and oil. Pour into a square pan and put into fridge for 60 minutes.
5. Slice into bars and keep chilled until ready to serve.

Nutrition Facts (per serving)
Calories 120
Net Carbs 1.4g
Fats 11.1g
Protein 2.4g
Fiber 2.6g

Lemon Sponge Cake

Makes 3

Ingredients
For Cake:
Baking powder (1 teaspoon)
Egg yolks (5)
Egg whites (5)
Almond extract (1 teaspoon)
Liquid stevia (1/4 teaspoon)
Olive oil (2 tablespoons)
Almond flour (1 cup)
Salt (1/4 teaspoon)
Vanilla (1 teaspoon)
Erythritol (1/4 cup)
Lemon zest (from 1/2 lemon)
Cream of tartar (1/2 teaspoon)
For Raspberry Icing:
Heavy cream (4 tablespoons)
Lemon juice (from 1/2 of a lemon)
Butter (4 tablespoons)
Raspberries (1/3 cup)

Directions
1. Set oven to 325 ̊F.
2. Combine all dry Ingredients except tartar and in another bowl mix together all wet Ingredients except zest and egg whites.
3. Add tartar to egg whites and beat until stiff peaks form.
4. Add egg white mix to cake batter and fold until thoroughly combined.
5. Grease cake pan and pour in batter; bake for 25 minutes.
6. Prepare icing by heating butter until golden then add lemon juice and cream, whisk and remove from heat.
7. Add raspberries and use spoon to crush as you combine mixture. Cool for 15 minutes. Pour on top of cakes before serving. Serve and enjoy.

Nutrition Facts (per serving)
Calories 414
Net Carbs 7.1g
Fats 38g
Protein 18g
Fiber 9.6g

Coffee Cake

Serves 8

Ingredients
For Cake:
Cream cheese (6 oz.)
Liquid stevia (1/4 teaspoon)
Vanilla extract (2 teaspoons)
Egg yolks (6)
Egg whites (6)
Erythritol (1/4 cup)
Protein powder (1/4 cup, unflavored)
Cream of tartar (1/4 teaspoon)
For filling:
Almond flour (1 1/2 cups)
Butter (1/2 stick)
Erythritol (1/4 cup)
Cinnamon (1 tablespoon)
Maple syrup (1/4 cup)

Directions
1. Set oven to 325 °F.
2. Add egg yolks to erythritol and beat together then add all Ingredients except egg white and tartar. Mix together to combine.
3. Combine tartar and white until peaks form.
4. Add half of egg whites to batter and fold in then add the remainder of egg whites and fold again.
5. Combine all filling Ingredients until dough like mixture if formed.
6. Add cake mixture to pan and top with as much of filling mixture as you can.
7. Bake for 20 minutes and top with leftover filling.
8. Bake for 20 minutes more, cool and serve.

Nutrition Facts (per serving)
Calories 257
Net Carbs 3.8g
Fats 26.7g
Protein 12.8g
Fiber 2.2g

Chocolate Dipped Macaroons

Makes 12

Ingredients
Coconut (1 cup, unsweetened and shredded)
Erythritol (1/4 cup)
Salt
Coconut oil (2 tablespoons)
Egg white (1)
Almond extract (1/2 teaspoon)
Chocolate (20 grams, sugar free)

Directions
1. Set oven to 350 F.
2. Line baking sheet with parchment paper and spread shredded coconut onto sheet; toast in oven for 5 minutes.
3. Beat the egg whites then add salt, almond extract and erythritol and beat again to combine.
4. Remove coconut from oven, cool and add to egg mixture.
5. Using a spoon or scoop, drop macaroons onto a lined baking sheet and bake for 15 minutes until golden.
6. Heat coconut oil until it melts in a saucepan then add chocolate and cook until it melts. Stir to avoid burning.
7. Dip macaroons into chocolate mixture and return to baking sheet to cool.
8. Serve.

Nutritional Facts
Calories 73
Net Carbs 1g
Fats 7.3g
Protein 1g
Fiber 1.7g

Spiced Lemon Glazed Fritters

Serves 6

Ingredients
Erythritol (3 tablespoons)
Egg (1)
Cinnamon (1/2 teaspoon)
Lemon zest (from 1/2 of lemon)
Almond flour (1/2 cup)
Baking powder (1 teaspoon)
Xanthan gum (1/2 teaspoon)
Vanilla (1/2 teaspoon)
Fat of choice (2 cups)

For glaze:
Erythritol (3 tablespoons, powder)
Lemon juice from 1/2 of lemon

Directions
1. Put all dry Ingredients for fritter into a bowl and mix together.
2. Add egg to dry mix and combine to form a sticky dough.
3. Heat oil in a deep pot and use spoon to drop fritters into hot oil. Fry fritters until golden.
4. Combine Ingredients for glaze until smooth and use to top fritters
5. Cool and serve.

Nutritional Facts
Calories 50
Net Carbs 0.7g
Fats 4.6g
Protein 1.7g
Fiber 7g

Cinnamon Bun Balls

Serves 8

Ingredients
1 cup coconut butter
1 cup full Fatcoconut milk (from a can)
1 cup unsweetened coconut shreds
1 tsp. vanilla extract
1/2 tsp. cinnamon
1/2 tsp. nutmeg
1 tsp. sugar substitute such as Splenda

Directions
1. Combine all Ingredients except the shredded coconut together in double boiler or a bowl set over a pan of simmering water. Stir until everything is melted and combined.
2. Remove bowl from heat and place in the fridge until the mixture has firmed up and can be rolled into balls.
3. Form the mixture into 1" balls, a small cookie scoop is helpful for doing this.
4. Roll each ball in the shredded coconut until well coated.
5. Serve and enjoy! Store in the fridge.

Nutritional Facts
Calories 42
Net Carbs 0.6g
Fats 4.6g
Protein 0.7g
Fiber 1g

Raspberry Cheesecake Cups

Serves 12

Ingredients
Almond meal (1/2 cup)
Stevia (1/2 cup)
Eggs (2)
Butter (4 tablespoons, melted)
Cream cheese (16 oz., softened)
Vanilla (1 teaspoon)
Raspberry syrup (1/4 cup, sugar free)

Directions
1. Set oven to 350 F and line baking molds.
2. Combine almond meal with melted butter and put into molds.
3. Add eggs, syrup, vanilla, cream cheese and Stevia to a bowl and use a hand mixer to cream mixture.
4. Use mixture to fill molds and bake for 15 minutes.
5. Remove from oven, cool for 10 minutes and refrigerate for 30 minutes.
6. Serve.

Nutritional Facts
Calories 206
Net Carbs 2.1g
Fats 19g
Protein 5g
Fiber 6g

Chocolate filled Fried Cookie Dough

Serves 12

Ingredients
Almond flour (3/4 cup)
Eggs (2)
Coconut oil (2 tablespoons)
Chocolate (3 squares)
Erythritol (1 teaspoon, powdered)
Casein powder (1 scoop, vanilla)
Stevia (10 drops)
Baking powder (1/2 tablespoon)
Granulated erythritol (2 teaspoons)

Directions
1. Combine almond flour, casein powder and baking powder.
2. Add granulated erythritol, stevia and egg to mixture and mix to combine until dough forms.
3. Form dough into a rectangular shape and slice into 12 pieces.
4. Chop each chocolate square into four parts. Take each slice of dough and make a well in the center of each.
5. Seal and roll into balls then heat oil in a frying pan.
6. Cook cookie balls until golden all over. Remove from pot, place on paper towels to remove excess oil.
7. Sprinkle with left over erythritol as they cool.
8. Serve.

Nutritional Facts
Calories 88
Net Carbs 1.9g
Fats 7.2g
Protein 4.7g
Fiber 12.8g

Coconut and Macadamia Custard

Makes 4

Ingredients
Eggs (4)
Macadamia Butter (1/3 cup)
Liquid stevia (1 teaspoon)
Coconut milk (1 cup, unsweetened)
Heavy cream (1/3 cup)
Vanilla (1 teaspoon)
Erythritol (1/3 cup)

Directions
1. Set oven to 325 F.
2. Place all Ingredients into a bowl and whisk together to combine. Be sure not to over mix the batter.
3. Add an inch of water to a baking pan and place ramekins into water. Divide batter equally amongst ramekins and bake for 40 minutes.
4. Cool for 45 minutes and place in refrigerator until ready to serve.

Nutritional Facts
Calories 88
Net Carbs 1.9g
Fats 7.2g
Protein 4.7g
Fiber 6.3g

Choco- Almond Butter Ice cream

Serves 6

Ingredients
Almond milk (1/2 cup)
Egg yolks (3)
Xanthan gum (1/4 teaspoon)
Chocolate chips (3/4 cup, sugar-free)
Heavy cream (1/2 cup)
Erythritol (1/4 cup)
Vanilla (1 teaspoon)
Vodka (1 tablespoon)
Almond butter (1/2 cup)

Directions
1. Add erythritol and cream to a saucepan and heat over a low flame until it starts to simmer.
2. Whisk vanilla and yolks together and add heated mixture a little at a time to eggs while whisking.
3. Return mixture to saucepan over a low flame and add gum to mixture, whisk until mixture thickens slightly.
4. Strain mixture through a fine sieve and add vodka. Refrigerate until chilled.
5. Process through an ice-cream machine according to the Directions.
6. Add Almond butter in the final second and freeze until ready to serve.
7. Enjoy.

Nutritional Facts
Calories 295
Net Carbs 5.8g
Fats 26g
Protein 8g
Fiber 2g

Jelly cookies

Makes 16

Ingredients
Coconut flour (2 tablespoons)
Cinnamon (1/4 teaspoon)
Erythritol (1/2 cup)
Coconut oil (4 tablespoons)
Almond extract (1/2 teaspoon)
Coconut (1 tablespoon, shredded)
Almond flour (1 cup)
Baking powder (1/2 teaspoon)
Salt (1/2 teaspoon)
Eggs (2)
Vanilla extract (1/2 teaspoon)
Jam of choice (2 tablespoons, sugar-free)

Directions
1. Set oven to 350°F.
2. Place all dry Ingredients in a bowl and whisk together to combine. Combine wet Ingredients and add to dry mix. Mix together until thoroughly combined.
3. Line a baking sheet with parchment paper and shape cookies on sheet. Make an indent in the center of each cookie.
4. Bake for 16 minutes until golden, remove from oven and cool.
5. Fill each indent with jam and coconut.
6. Serve.

Nutritional Facts
Calories 86
Net Carbs 1.2g
Fats 7.9g
Protein 2.4g
Fiber 1.3g

Almond Butter Truffles

Makes 12

Ingredients
Almond butter (1 cup)
Erythritol (1 ½ cups, powdered)
Butter (4 tablespoons, melted)
Chocolate (6 oz., sugar-free)

Directions
1. Combine erythritol, butter and Almond butter in a bowl until mixture binds together.
2. Roll batter into balls and place on a lined baking sheet. Refrigerate for 30 minutes or until very cold.
3. Melt chocolate in a saucepan and check consistency, should be thick enough to stick to truffles.
4. Use a spoon to dip truffles into melted chocolate, coat all sides of truffles.
5. Refrigerate to set and serve.

Nutritional Facts
Calories 200
Net Carbs 5g
Fats 17g
Protein 5.9g
Fiber 3g

Lava Cake

Makes 1

Ingredients
Erythritol (2 tablespoons)
Heavy cream (1 tablespoon)
Baking powder (1/4 teaspoon)
Cocoa powder (2 tablespoons)
Egg (1)
Vanilla (1/2 teaspoon)
Salt

Directions
1. Set oven to 350 °F.
2. Combine cocoa powder with erythritol in a bowl and in another bowl whisk egg until fluffy.
3. Add vanilla, cream, baking powder, salt and egg to cocoa mix.
4. Grease a ramekin and add batter to it; bake for 14 minutes. Do not bake too much; cake should not be too firm.
5. Serve.

Nutritional Facts
Calories 173
Net Carbs 4g
Fats 13g
Protein 8g
Fiber 5g

Creamy Pistachio Strawberry Popsicles

Makes 4

Ingredients
Pistachios (2 oz., salted)
Almond milk (1/2 cup)
Strawberries (8 oz.)
Heavy cream (1/2 cup)
Stevia (15 drops)

Directions
1. Put strawberries in a processor along with milk, stevia and cream. Pulse until all Ingredients are combined.
2. Add pistachios and fold in; do not blend.
3. Pour mixture into Popsicle molds and freeze for 3 hours or more.
4. Serve.

Nutritional Facts
Calories 158
Net Carbs 5.6g
Fats 12.5g
Protein 4g
Fiber 3g

Lemony Cheesecake Mousse

Serves 5

Ingredients
Lemon juice (1/4 cup)
Lemon stevia (1 teaspoon, liquid)
Mascarpone cheese (8 oz.)
Salt (1/8 teaspoon)
Heavy cream (1 cup)

Directions
1. Add lemon juice and cheese to a bowl and use a hand mixer to combine until smooth.
2. Add lemon juice, salt and cream to mixture and whip until fluffy.
3. Pipe mixture into glasses and top with zest.
4. Chill and serve.

Nutritional Facts
Calories 277
Net Carbs 1.7g
Fats 29.6g
Protein 3.7g
Fiber 0g

Macchiato Cheesecake

Serves 9

Ingredients
For Cheesecake Base
Butter (2 tablespoons, unsalted)
Caramel syrup (1 tablespoon, sugar-free)
Cream cheese (8 oz., soft)
Espresso concentrate (3 tablespoons, cold)
Stevia (1/3 cup)
For frosting:
Caramel syrup (3 tablespoons, sugar free)
Mascarpone cheese (8 oz., soft)
Butter (3 tablespoons, unsalted, softened)
Splenda (2 tablespoons)

Directions
1. Set oven to 350°F.
2. Place all Ingredients for cheesecake in a bowl and use a mixer to blend together until smooth.
3. Grease cupcake pan and add batter; bake for 15 minutes.
4. Take from oven, cool and refrigerate for 3 hours or more.
5. Prepare frosting by add all Ingredients to a bowl and using a mixer to cream. Be sure to cream on low speed.
6. Top cakes with frosting and serve.

Nutritional Facts
Calories 286
Net Carbs 1g
Fats 29g
Protein 5g
Fiber 3g

Lemon and Blackberry Mini Tarts

Makes 10

Ingredients
For crust:
Egg (1)
Coconut (3/4 cup, shredded)
Macadamia nuts (1 cup)
For filling:
Lemon juice from ½ lemon
Erythritol (1/4 cup)
Gelatin powder (1 ½ tablespoons)
Coconut milk (1 cup)
Lemon zest (1 tablespoon)
Stevia (15 drops)
Water (3 tablespoons)
For Topping:
Blackberries (1 cup)

Directions
1. Set oven to 400 ℉.
2. Add coconut milk to a saucepan along with stevia, erythritol and lemon zest. Stir together, heat but do not boil and take from heat.
3. Combine gelatin with water and add to mixture in pot. Mix together until thoroughly combined; put aside to cool and thicken.
4. Crush nuts in a processor to desired consistency and then add to a bowl. Pulse coconut and add to nuts then add egg and mix together until mixture binds together.
5. Line a cupcake tin with paper liners and press base into each mold. Bake for 7 minutes and take from oven.
6. Top with filling and blackberries and refrigerate for 30 minutes or more. Serve

Nutritional Facts
Calories 178
Net Carbs 2.8g
Fats 16.2g
Protein 4.4g
Fiber 3.1g

Lemon Soufflés

Makes 4

Ingredients
Eggs (2)
Lemon zest (2 teaspoons)
Vanilla (1 teaspoon)
Ricotta (1 cup, whole milk)
Erythritol (1/4 cup)
Lemon juice (1 tablespoon, fresh)
Poppy seeds (1 teaspoon)

Directions
1. Set oven to 375°F.
2. Separate eggs and add 2 tablespoons erythritol to whites and beat until stiff peaks start to form.
3. Add remaining erythritol to egg yolks along with ricotta cheese and beat until mixture is creamy.
4. Add lemon juice and zest to cheese mixture, stir and add poppy seeds and vanilla.
5. Add egg whites a little at a time to ricotta mixture and fold to combine.
6. Grease ramekins and fill with soufflé mixture. Shake containers to level the soufflés.
7. Bake for 20 minutes.
8. Serve.

Nutritional Facts
Calories 151
Net Carbs 2.9g
Fats 10.8g
Protein 9g
Fiber 0g

Caramel Pots

Serves 4

Ingredients
Heavy cream (1 ½ cups)
Liquid stevia (1/4 teaspoon)
Egg yolks (4)
Maple syrup (1 tablespoon)
Maple extract (1 teaspoon)
Erythritol (1/4 cup, powdered)
Salt (1/4 teaspoon)
Water (6 tablespoons)
Vanilla extract (1/2 teaspoon)

Directions
1. Set oven to 300 ℉.
2. Combine water and erythritol in a saucepan and heat until mixture starts to boil. Add maple syrup and mix together. Boil for 3 minutes until mixture reduces and is syrupy.
3. Add cream, maple extract, sat, stevia and vanilla to another saucepan. Bring to a boil then lower heat and add erythritol mixture slowly while stirring.
4. Add mixture a little at a time to egg yolks and mix thoroughly. You may strain the mixture if you choose to.
5. Fill a baking pan large enough to hold your ramekins with about an inch of water. Place ramekins into pan and add mixture to ramekins.
6. Bake for 40 minutes.
7. Serve warm or cold.

Nutritional Facts
Calories 359
Net Carbs 3g
Fats 34.9g
Protein 2.8g
Fiber 0g

Whisky Vanilla Mug Cake

Serves 1-2

Ingredients
Egg (1)
Almond flour (3 tablespoons)
Stevia (7 drops)
Whisky (1 tablespoon)
Coconut flour (2 teaspoons)
Butter (2 tablespoons)
Erythritol (1 tablespoon)
Baking powder (1/2 teaspoon)
Vanilla (1/2 teaspoon)

Directions
1. Combine all Ingredients in a microwave safe mug until thoroughly combined.
2. Place in microwave for 2 minutes.
3. Serve in mug or turn upside down and remove from mug onto a plate.
4. Enjoy.

Nutritional Facts
Calories 448
Net Carbs 5g
Fats 40g
Protein 12g
Fiber 4g

Maple Pecan Muffins

Serves 5

Ingredients
Flaxseed (1/2 cup)
Coconut oil (1/2 cup)
Erythritol (1/4 cup)
Vanilla extract (1 teaspoon)
Apple cider vinegar (1/2 teaspoon)
Almond flour (1 cup)
Pecans (3/4 cup)
Eggs (2)
Maple extract (2 teaspoons)
Baking soda (1/2 teaspoon)
Stevia (1/4 teaspoon, liquid)

Directions
1. Set oven to 325 ℉.
2. Put pecan in a processor and pulse until chopped. Transfer to a large bowl reserving 1/3 of pecans until needed.
3. Add remaining dry Ingredients to pecans and combine liquids together in another bowl. Add wet Ingredients to dry mix and combine.
4. Line cupcake pan/muffin tin and add batter then top with reserved pecans.
5. Bake for 30 minutes, remove and cool.
6. Serve.

Nutritional Facts
Calories 208
Net Carbs 1.5g
Fats 20.7g
Protein 4.8g
Fiber 2.8g

Chocolate Blackberry Panna Cotta

Serves 10

Ingredients
Cream cheese (12 oz.)
Butter (3 tablespoons)
Erythritol (2 tablespoons)
Gelatin powder (2 ½ teaspoons)
Water (1 cup)
Blackberry preserves (3 tablespoons +1 teaspoon)
Cocoa powder (3 tablespoons)
Vanilla (1 teaspoon)
Liquid stevia (10 drops)

Directions
1. Place softened butter, vanilla and cream cheese in a bowl and use mixer to cream mixture.
2. Heat water and combine with erythritol and gelatin then add to cream cheese mixture.
3. Carefully blend mixture until creamy and smooth then add cocoa and blend again.
4. Grease cupcake molds and pour in batter; place in fridge for 20 minutes.
5. Divide preserves amongst panna cotta and stir to combine. Return to fridge and set overnight.
6. Serve.

Nutritional Facts
Calories 156.2
Net Carbs 24.5g
Fats 15.8g
Protein 2.9g
Fiber 1.6g

Snicker doodle Cookies

Makes 14

Ingredients
For cookies:
Coconut oil (1/4 cup)
Vanilla (1 tablespoon)
Liquid Stevia (7 drops)
Macadamia nuts (1/3 cup)
Almond flour (2 cups)
Maple syrup (1/4 cup)
Baking soda (1/4 teaspoon)
Salt

For topping:
Erythritol (2 tablespoons)
Cinnamon (2 tablespoons)

Directions
1. Set oven to 350 °F.
2. Combine salt, baking soda and flour in a large bowl.
3. In another container combine maple syrup, stevia, oil and vanilla. Crush nuts in a processor.
4. Add wet Ingredients to dry and mix together. Combine Ingredients for topping in another container.
5. Form dough into balls, roll in toppings mixture and place on a lined baking sheet.
6. Flatten and bake cookies for 10 minutes.
7. Cool and serve.

Nutritional Facts
Calories 155
Net Carbs 2.1g
Fats 14.8g
Protein 3.6g
Fiber 2.5g

Chocolate Almond Cookies

Servings: 12

Ingredients
2 cups almond meal
1 1/2 tsp. almond extract
4 Tbsp. cocoa powder
5 Tbsp. coconut oil, melted
2 Tbsp. almond milk
4 Tbsp. agave nectar
2 tsp. vanilla extract
1/8 tsp. baking soda
1/8 tsp. salt

Directions
1. Preheat oven to 340F degrees.
2. In a deep bowl mix salt, cocoa powder, almond meal and baking soda.
3. In a separate bowl, whisk together melted coconut oil, almond milk, almond and vanilla extract and maple syrup. Merge the almond meal mixture with almond milk mixture and mix well.
4. In a greased baking pan pour the batter evenly. Bake for 10-15 minutes. 5. Once ready let cool on a wire rack and serve.

Nutritional Facts
Calories 79.32g
Net Carbs 2.1g
Fats 5.94g
Protein 0.46g
Fiber 0.61g

Lemon & Coconut Balls

Serves 4

Ingredients
3 packages of True Lemon (Crystallized Citrus for Water)
1/4 cup shredded coconut, unsweetened
1 cup cream cheese
1/4 cup granulated Stevia

Directions
1. In a bowl, combine cream cheese, lemon and Stevia. Blend well until incorporate.
2. Once the mixture is well combined, put it back in the fridge to harden up a bit.
3. Roll into 16 balls and dip each ball into shredded coconut. Refrigerate for several hours. Serve.

Nutritional Facts
Calories 216
Net Carbs 3.12g
Fats 21.50g
Protein 3.61g
Fiber 0.45g

Chocolate Chia Cream

Serves 4

Ingredients
1/4 cup Chia seeds
1 cup heavy whipping cream
1 cup coconut milk
2 Tbsp. cocoa powder
Pure vanilla extract
1/4 cup Erythritol sweetener

Directions
1. In a bowl mix the chia seeds and add the coconut milk until it combines well.
2. Add the Erythritol and whisk some more. Divide the mixture into two portions.
3. Add cocoa to one half and mixed it nicely.
4. Pour chia seed mixture into the bowls or glasses. Keep covered in the refrigerator for 12 hours.
5. Before serving beat the heavy whipping cream and pour over the chia seeds cream. Enjoy!

Nutritional Facts
Calories 341,31
Net Carbs 7.35g
Fats 35.41g
Protein 2.99g
Fiber 1.56g

Almond Butter Delights

Serves: 16

Ingredients
2 eggs
2 1/2 cup of peanut butter
1/2 cup shredded coconut (unsweetened)
1/2 cup of Xylitol
1 Tbsp. of pure vanilla extract

Directions
1. Preheat oven to 320 F.
2. Mix all Ingredients together by your hands.
3. After the Ingredients are thoroughly mixed, roll into heaped tablespoon sized balls and press into a baking tray lined with baking paper.
4. Bake in the oven for 12 minutes or until the tops of the cookies are browning. When ready, let cool on a wire rack. Ready!
5. Serve.

Nutritional Facts
Calories 254
Net Carbs 8.31g
Fats 21.75g
Protein 10.98g
Fiber 2.64g

Creamy Lemon Bombs

Serves: 10

Ingredients
1/2 cup cream cheese
1/2 cup coconut oil
1/2 cup heavy whipping cream
1 tsp. pure lemon extract
10 drops sweetener of choice

Directions
1. With help of an immersion blender, blend together all of the Ingredients.
2. Spread the mixture into a silicone tray and freeze for 2-3 hours.
3. Once hardened, remove from the silicone tray and serve. Enjoy!

Nutrition Facts (per serving)
Carbs: 0,9g
Fiber: 0g
Net Carbs: 0,47g
Protein: 0,93g
Fat: 19,27g
Calories: 175

Cream Cheese Balls

Serves: 8

Ingredients
1 cup cream cheese
1/4 cup coconut butter
1 package of sugar free jello

Directions
1. In a small bowl put the jello powder.
2. In a separate bowl, mix together cream cheese and coconut butter.
3. Take a teaspoon of batter, roll into a ball in your hands and then roll in the jello powder. Make 16 balls.
4. Cover with plastic wrap and place in the fridge.

Nutrition Facts (per serving)
Carbs: 1,20g
Fiber: 0g
Net Carbs: 1g
Protein: 2g
Fat: 16g
Calories: 150g

Gingery Bomb

Serves: 10

Ingredients
1 tsp. dried (powdered) ginger
0.8 oz shredded coconut (unsweetened)
1/3 cup coconut oil, softened
1/3 cup coconut butter, softened
1 tsp. granulated sweetener of choice, to taste

Directions
1. In a deep bowl, mix shredded coconut, coconut oil, coconut butter, sweetener and dried powdered ginger.
2. Pour the ginger mixture into ice block trays and refrigerate for 1 hour to solidify.

Nutrition Facts (per serving)
Carbs: 2,5g
Fiber: 0,25g
Net Carbs: 0,3g
Protein: 2
Fat: 14,5g
Calories: 134

Almond Butter Fudge

Serves: 12

Ingredients
1 cup natural almond butter
1 cup coconut oil
1/4 cup almond milk, unsweetened
1 tsp. vanilla extract
2 tsp. liquid sweetener of your choice (optional)
pinch of coarse sea salt

Directions
1. Line 9X4" loaf pan with parchment paper
2. In a microwave safe bowl, soften the almond butter and coconut oil together about one minute.
3. Combine the softened almond butter and coconut oil with the remaining Ingredients into a blender.
4. Blend until thoroughly combined. Pour the batter into prepared loaf pan.
5. Refrigerate about two hours. Serve!

Nutrition Facts (per serving)
Carbs: 4,25g
Fiber: 1,29g
Net Carbs: 2,03g
Protein: 5,39g
Fat: 29g
Calories: 284

Spicy Chocolate Bombs

Serves: 12

Ingredients
3/4 cup melted coconut oil
3/4 cup melted salted butter
3/4 cup almond butter
1/4 cup cocoa powder
4 Tbsp. liquid sweetener of your choice
pinch of cayenne pepper

Directions
1. Stir all Ingredients in a big bowl and mix well together.
2. Put the mixture into small cake holders (cupcake, muffin, etc).
3. Put into the freezer for half an hour.
4. You can also keep your bombs in the freezer if you want.

Nutrition Facts (per serving)
Carbs: 1,8g
Fiber: 0,6g
Net Carbs: 0,04g
Protein: 0,53g
Fat: 23,35g
Calories: 270

Vanilla Muffin Bombs

Serves: 6

Ingredients
8 oz cream cheese, softened
1/2 cup heavy whipping cream
2 Tbsp. coconut butter, melted
1/2 cup sweetener of your choice to taste
1 1/2 tsp. vanilla extract
dash of sea salt

Directions
1. In a blender add all Ingredients for 2-3 minutes. Consistency should be mousse like.
2. Blend until combined.
3. With blender running, slowly add the heavy cream.
4. Prepare a muffin tin with 6 paper liners and divide the mixture into the cups.
5. Chill in the fridge for 2-3 hours. Serve.

Nutrition Facts (per serving)
Carbs: 2,23g
Fiber: 0g
Net Carbs: 1,37g
Protein: 2,67g
Fat: 22,2g
Calories: 217

Fresh Basil Coco Balls

Serves: 6

Ingredients
1/2 cup coconut oil melted
2 Tbsp. almond butter, melted
2 Tbsp. cocoa powder
2 Tbsp. sweetener of your choice, to taste
2 Tbsp. basil leaves (fresh, finely chopped)

Directions
1. Mix the melted coconut oil and almond butter with the finely chopped basil leaves and sweetener.
2. Pour half the mixture into silicon cases or ice cube trays. Place in the fridge.
3. Add the cocoa powder to the remaining mixture, then pour onto the coconut oil layer which has set in the fridge.
4. Keep refrigerated until set completely.

Nutrition Facts (per serving)
Carbs: 1,12g
Fiber: 0,64g
Net Carbs: 0,03g
Protein: 0,41g
Fat: 22,26g
Calories: 195

Choc Chip Almond Butter Cups

Serves: 8

Ingredients
1/2 cup of peanut butter, room temperature
1/4 cup of butter, softened
1/4 cup of coconut oil, room temperature
4 Tbsp. of heavy whipping cream
1 cup of dark unsweetened chocolate chips/cacao nibs

Directions
1. In a bowl, melt together chocolate chips and heavy whipping cream.
2. Drop a spoonful of melted chocolate mixture into mold and tilt to cover bottom and sides.
3. When you finish filling, pop into the freezer to set, about 20 minutes.
4. In a meanwhile, whip together peanut butter, coconut oil and butter.
5. Remove hardened molds from freezer and plop a spoonful of the almond butter mixture into the centers of each one and smooth it out.
6. Top those with a spoonful of the remaining chocolate and pop them back to the freezer for at least a half hour. Ready!

Nutrition Facts (per serving)
Carbs: 14,58g
Fiber: 2,21g
Net Carbs: 1,5g
Protein: 5,06g
Fat: 23,27g
Calories: 317

Almond Vanilla Ice-cream

Serves: 10

Ingredients
1/3 cup cocoa butter, melted
1/3 cup coconut oil, melted
4 Tbsp. almond butter
4 eggs
4 yolks
1/3 cup natural vanilla flavor
1 cup sweetener of your choice
2 tsp. vanilla bean powder
8-10 ice cubes

Directions
1. Add all Ingredients but ice cubes into blender and pulse on HIGH for 2 minutes.
2. While the blender is still running, remove the top portion of the lid and drop in 1 ice cube at a time, allowing the blender to run about 10 seconds between each ice cube. Transfer the mixture to 9x5 loaf pan and place in the freezer for 3-4 hours.
3. Serve immediately as soft-serve or scoop into a 9x5 loaf pan and freeze for 45 minutes.

Nutrition Facts (per serving)
Carbs: 4,13g
Fiber: 0g
Net Carbs: 3,51g
Protein: 3,7g
Fat: 22,16g
Calories: 234

Chocolate Almond Butter

Serves: 12

Ingredients
4 Tbsp. almond butter
4 Tbsp. butter
4 Tbsp. coconut oil (refined)
2 Tbsp. cocoa powder, unsweetened
24 drops sweetener of your choice

Directions
1. Melt butter in microwave
2. In a bowl, add coconut oil, almond butter and cocoa powder.
3. Add sweetener to taste. Blend well.
4. Pour into molds and freeze for 30 minutes.
5. Serve.

Nutrition Facts (per serving)
Carbs: 0,53g
Fiber: 0,3g
Net Carbs: 0,02g
Protein: 0,26g
Fat: 12,34g
Calories: 109

Spicy Coconut Balls

Serves: 12

Ingredients
1 cup coconut butter
1 cup coconut milk
1/2 tsp. cinnamon
1 cup coconut shreds
1 tsp. vanilla extract
1/2 tsp. nutmeg
1 tsp. sweetener powder extract (of your choice)

Directions
1. Place all the Ingredients except shredded coconut in a double boiler over medium heat.
2. Mix the Ingredients while waiting for them to melt.
3. When all the Ingredients are combined remove the bowl from the heat.
4. Place the ball in a fridge about one hour.
5. Make balls and roll them through the coconut shreds.
6. Place the balls on a plate and refrigerate for one hour.
7. Serve and enjoy.

Nutrition Facts (per serving)
Carbs: 2,32g
Fiber: 0,68g
Net Carbs: 0,5g
Protein: 0,71g
Fat: 21,77g
Calories: 201

Coconut Truffles

Serves: 8

Ingredients
3 cups coconut, unsweetened, shredded
6 Tbsp. coconut oil
1 cup sweetener of your choice
2 tsp. vanilla
pinch of salt (optional)

<u>Toppings:</u>
coconut shreds; chopped nuts, etc.

Directions
1. Put all Ingredients in a food processor or blender.
2. Combine until the mixture is blended and sticks together.
3. Remove the mixture from the blender / food processor and form into balls.
4. Decorate with shredded coconut, cocoa, crushed nuts...etc.
5. Leave to firm up on a plate or refrigerate for 30 minutes.
6. Serve.

Nutrition Facts (per serving)
Carbs: 14,06g
Fiber: 2,7g
Net Carbs: 10,48g
Protein: 1,23g
Fat: 22,16g
Calories: 253

Coconut Dream Bonbons

Serves: 20

Ingredients
Candies
1/2 cup shredded coconut, unsweetened
1/2 cup coconut butter
1/2 cup coconut oil
3 Tbsp. sweetener of your choice, to taste
Topping
1/4 cup cocoa butter
1/4 cup cocoa powder
3 oz Sugar-free dark chocolate
1/4 cup powdered sweetener of your choice (optional)
1/4 tsp. vanilla extract

Directions
1. Line a mini-muffin pan with 20 mini paper nonstick liners.
2. In a saucepan, combine coconut butter and coconut oil over low heat. Stir until melted and smooth. Stir in shredded coconut and sweetener until combined.
3. Divide mixture among prepared mini muffin cups and freeze about 30 minutes.
4. For the chocolate coating, combine cocoa butter and unsweetened chocolate together in bowl set over a pan of simmering water (do not let the bottom of the bowl touch the water). Stir until melted.
5. Stir in sifted powdered sweetener, then stir in cocoa powder, until smooth. Remove from heat and stir in vanilla extract.
6. Melt dark chocolate and spoon over the cold coconut filling.
7. Candies can be stored on your counter top for up to a week.

Nutrition Facts (per serving)
Carbs: 3,75
Fiber: 0,58g
Net Carbs: 0,19g
Protein: 0,52g
Fat: 15,56g
Calories: 142

Choc - Fraise Strawberry Treats

Serves: 12

Ingredients
1/3 cup coconut butter
1/2 cup coconut oil
1/2 Tbsp. cocoa powder
10 drops of liquid sweetener of your choice
1/3 cup fresh strawberries, diced
1 Tbsp. coconut, unsweetened shredded
water

Directions
1. In a pan placed over the container holding hot water (bain-marie), add the coconut butter, 1/3 cup coconut oil, cocoa powder and a few drops of liquid sweetener of your choice. Heat and stir until fully melted.
2. In a small saucepan, add the fresh strawberries and a few spoonful's of water. Cook over medium heat until soft. Mash the strawberries with a fork.
3. Add the mashed strawberries to a blender with 1 Tbsp. of melted coconut oil and a few more drops of liquid sweetener of your choice. Blend until smooth.
4. Fill molds with the melted coconut mixture. Add about 1 tsp. of the strawberry mixture into each mold. Sprinkle with a few shreds of coconut.
5. Refrigerate for a couple of hours. Serve and enjoy!!

Nutrition Facts (per serving)
Carbs: 0,52g
Fiber: 0,2g
Net Carbs: 0,24g
Protein: 0,14g
Fat: 14,38g
Calories: 126

Decadent Lime Squares

Serves: 8

Ingredients
1/4 cup cream cheese
1/4 cup heavy cream
1/4 butter
2 Tbsp. virgin coconut oil
1 lime, squeezed
1 tsp. lime extract
sweetener to taste

Directions
1. In a bowl, mix melted cream cheese, butter and coconut oil; whisk until blended. Add the heavy cream and whisk.
2. Squeeze in lime juice and the lime extract. Add sweetener of your choice per taste.
3. Carefully pour into your tray and leave in your freezer overnight.
4. Pop them out of the tray the next morning, Ready! Enjoy!

Nutrition Facts (per serving)
Carbs: 0,67g
Fiber: 0,01g
Net Carbs: 0,28g
Protein: 0,62g
Fat: 11,51
Calories: 105

Coconut Melon Squares

Serves: 12

Ingredients
1 cup coconut butter
1/2 cup melon cubes
1/2 tsp. sweetener of your choice to taste
1/2 tsp. vanilla extract
1 Tbsp. lemon juice

Directions
1. Line a small pan with parchment paper. Set aside.
2. Place melon cubes, coconut butter and coconut oil in a pot and heat over medium heat until well combined. When ready, set aside to cool for 10 minutes.
3. In a blender, add melon mix and remaining Ingredients. Blend until smooth.
4. Spread out into a prepared pan. Refrigerate until mix has hardened.
5. Remove from fridge and cut into squares. Serve.

Nutrition Facts (per serving)
Carbs: 0,81g
Fiber: 006g
Net Carbs: 0,65g
Protein: 0,21g
Fat: 15,38g
Calories: 139,11

Dark Chocolate Cups

Serves: 4

Ingredients
4 Tbsp. coconut oil (refined)
4 Tbsp. dark chocolate cocoa powder
3 tsp. sweetener of your choice
1 tsp. vanilla extract
Almond butter
Sea salt (optional)

Directions
1. Melt coconut oil in microwave for 45 seconds. In a bowl, stir in cocoa, sweetener of your choice and vanilla; mix until smooth.
2. Pour chocolate mixture into mini silicone cups and spoon a small bit of Almond butter into each cup. Sprinkle with sea salt (optional).
3. Freeze for 30 minutes. Ready for enjoy!

Nutrition Facts (per serving)
Carbs: 5,55g
Fiber: 1,8g
Net Carbs: 2,3g
Protein: 1,11g
Fat: 14,34
Calories: 141

Pure Coconut Squares

Serves: 10

Ingredients
6 Tbsp. cocoa butter, softened
6 Tbsp. coconut oil melted
2 Tbsp. finely shredded coconut
1 tsp. granulated sweetener of choice, to taste

Directions
1. In a bowl, mix all the Ingredients in a pouring bowl.
2. Pour into ice cube trays or silicon moulds.
3. Refrigerate for 30 minutes.
4. Serve!

Nutrition Facts (per serving)
Carbs: 2,12 g
Fiber: 0,02g
Net Carbs: 0,1g
Protein: 0,05g
Fat: 19,04g
Calories: 174

Soft Raspberry Bombs

Serves: 10

Ingredients
1/2 cup cream cheese, at room temperature
1/2 cup coconut oil
1/2 cup heavy whipping cream
1 tsp. pure raspberry extract
10 drops sweetener of choice

Directions
1. With help of an immersion blender, blend together all of the Ingredients.
2. Spread the mixture into a silicone tray and freeze for 2-3 hours.
3. Once hardened, remove from the silicone tray and serve.
4. Enjoy!

Nutrition Facts (per serving)
Carbs: 0,89g
Fiber: 0g
Net Carbs: 0,47g
Protein: 0,93g
Fat: 19,27g
Calories: 175

Vanilla Coconut Cakes

Serves: 24

Ingredients
4 oz cacao butter
2 cup coconut milk
1/2 cup coconut oil
1 cup coconut butter
1/2 cup vanilla protein powder
1 tsp. pure vanilla extract
1 tsp. liquid sweetener of your choice
pinch salt (optional)
unsweetened coconut flakes

Directions
1. Line the 8 by 8 pan with parchment paper.
2. Melt the cacao butter in a sauce pan over low heat.
3. Stir in the coconut oil, coconut butter and coconut milk; stir well until completely smooth.
4. Turn off heat and whisk in the sweetener of your taste, pure vanilla extract, protein powder and salt.
5. Pour mixture into prepared pan.
6. Sprinkle with coconut flakes.
7. Refrigerate overnight.
8. Enjoy!

Nutrition Facts (per serving)
Carbs: 1,14g
Fiber: 0g
Net Carbs: 0,03g
Protein: 0,4g
Fat: 21,1g
Calories: 189,64

Soft & Creamy Orange Squares

Serves: 10

Ingredients
1/2 cup cream cheese (heavy cream)
1/2 cup coconut oil
1/2 cup heavy whipping cream
1 tsp. pure orange extract
10 drops sweetener of choice

Directions
1. With help of an immersion blender, blend together all of the Ingredients.
2. Spread the mixture into a silicone tray and freeze for 2-3 hours.
3. Once hardened, remove from the silicone tray and serve.
4. Enjoy!

Nutrition Facts (per serving)
Carbs: 0,89g
Fiber: 0g
Protein: 0,93g
Fat: 19,27
Calories: 175

Strawberry Walnut Bombs

Serves: 8

Ingredients
1/3 cup butter
4 Tbsp. coconut oil
2 Tbsp. sugar-free strawberry syrup
3 Tbsp. walnuts, ground
2 Tbsp. cocoa powder

Directions
1. Combine all Ingredients (except ground walnuts) in sauce pan over extremely low heat until chocolate sauce consistency.
2. Make 8 bowls and roll in ground walnuts.
3. Place balls on a serving pan and freeze for at least 2 hours.

Nutrition Facts (per serving)
Carbs: 1,17g
Fiber: 0,64g
Protein: 0,77g
Fat: 16,49g
Calories: 147

Watermelon Soup

Serves 1

Ingredients
Watermelon (3/4 cups, seeds removed)
Sour cream (2 tablespoons)
Lemon juice (1/4 teaspoon)
Heavy cream (1/2 cup, whipped)
Raspberries (1/4 cup)
Vanilla Stevia (1 tablespoon)
Mint (1/4 teaspoon, fresh, chopped)

Directions
1. Add all Ingredients except whipped cream to a blender and pulse until thoroughly combined.
2. Pour into a bowl and top with cream.
3. Serve.

Nutritional Facts
Calories 192
Net Carbs 8g
Fats 17g
Protein 2g
Fiber 1g

Delicious Nuts Bars

Serves 10

Ingredients
1 cup almonds
1/2 cup hazelnut, chopped
1 cup peanuts
1 cup shredded coconut
1 cup almond butter
1 cup Liquid Erythritol
1 cup coconut oil, freshly melted and still warm

Directions
1. In a food processor place all nuts and chop for 1-2 minutes.
2. Add in grated coconut, almond butter, Erythritol and coconut oil. Process it for 1 minute about.
3. Cover a square bowl with parchment paper and place the mixture on top.
4. Flatten the mixture with a spatula. Place the bowl in the freezer for 4-5 hours.
5. Remove batter from the freezer, cut and serve.

Nutritional Facts
Calories 193,62
Net Carbs 5.4g
Fats 18,2g
Protein 3.38g
Fiber 2.53g

Sticky Chocolate Fudge Squares

Serves 12

Ingredients
1 cup coconut oil, softened
1/4 cup coconut milk (full fat, from a can)
1/4 cup cocoa powder
1 teaspoon vanilla extract
1/2 teaspoon sea salt
1-3 drops liquid stevia

Directions
1. With a hand mixer or stand mixer, whip the softened coconut oil and coconut milk together until smooth and glossy. About 6 minutes on high.
2. Add the cocoa powder, vanilla extract, sea salt, and one drop of liquid stevia to the bowl and mix on low until combined. Increase speed once everything is combined and mix for one minute. Taste fudge and adjust sweetness by adding additional liquid stevia, if desired.
3. Prepare a 9"x4" loaf pan by lining it with parchment paper.
4. Pour fudge into loaf pan and place in freezer for about 15, until just set.
5. Remove fudge and cut into 1" x 1" pieces. Store in an airtight container in the fridge or freezer.

Nutritional Facts
Calories 172
Net Carbs 5.4g
Fats 19,6g
Protein 3.38g
Fiber 2.53g

Coco - Raspberry Delights

Serves 12

Ingredients
1/2 cup coconut butter
1/2 cup coconut oil
1/2 cup freeze dried raspberries
1/2 cup unsweetened shredded coconut
1/4 powdered sugar substitute such as Swerve or Truvia

Directions
1. Line an 8"x8" pan with parchment paper.
2. In a food processor, coffee grinder, or blender, pulse the dried raspberries into a fine powder.
3. In a saucepan over medium heat, combine the coconut butter, coconut oil, coconut, and sweetener. Stir until melted and well combined.
4. Remove pan from heat and stir in raspberry powder.
5. Pour mixture into pan and refrigerate or freeze for several hours, or overnight.
6. Cut into 12 pieces and serve!

Nutritional Facts
Calories 234
Net Carbs 1.1g
Fats 23.6g
Protein 3.9g
Fiber 3.8g

Blueberry Power

Serves 6

Ingredients
5 Tbsp. butter
3 Tbsp. coconut oil
2 Tbsp. sugar-free Blueberry syrup
2 Tbsp. cocoa powder

Directions
1. In a sauce pan add all Ingredients and cook over low heat until chocolate sauce texture.
2. Pour into mold and freeze for at least 3 hours.
3. Before serving unmold and enjoy.

Nutritional Facts
Calories 148
Net Carbs 0.05g
Fats 17g
Protein 0.5g
Fiber 0.6g

Chia and Pecan Butter Blondie's

Makes 16

Ingredients
Pecans (2 ¼ cups, roasted)
Butter (1/4 cup, melted)
Salted caramel (3 tablespoons, sugar free)
Eggs (3)
Heavy cream (3 tablespoons)
Chia seeds (1/2 cup, ground)
Erythritol (1/4 cup, powdered)
Liquid stevia (10 drops)
Baking powder (1 teaspoon)
Salt (to taste)

Directions
1. Set oven to 350 ℉.
2. Spread pecan on a baking sheet and roast for 10-15 minutes until fragrant.
3. Put chia seeds in a grinder and grind finely; grind erythritol and combine with chia seeds in a bowl.
4. Process 2/3 of pecans to form butter, reserve the remaining pecans until needed.
5. Add eggs, nut butter, salt and stevia to chia mixture; mix together until thoroughly combined.
6. Add caramel, heavy cream, melted and baking powder to mixture and mix together then add leftover pecans and fold.
7. Grease a baking pan (square) and add batter.
8. Bake for 20 minutes, remove from oven and cool.
9. Slice and serve.

Nutritional Facts
Calories 174
Net Carbs 1.1g
Fats 17.1g
Protein 3.9g
Fiber 3.8g

Neapolitan Bombs

Makes 24

Ingredients
Butter (1/2 cup)
Sour cream (1/2 cup)
Cocoa powder (2 tablespoons)
Liquid Stevia (25 drops)
Strawberries (2)
Coconut oil (1/2 cup)
Cream cheese (1/2 cup)
Erythritol (2 tablespoons)
Vanilla (1 teaspoon)

Directions
1. Place all Ingredients into a blender except strawberries, vanilla and cocoa powder. Pulse until mixture is thoroughly combined.
2. Split mixture into three parts and add strawberries to one and mash to combine. Add vanilla to another and cocoa to the final mixture.
3. Pour cocoa mixture into mold and put into freezer for 30 minutes. Remove and repeat with two remaining mixtures.
4. Freeze for an hour or more and serve.

Nutritional Facts
Calories 102
Net Carbs 0.4g
Fats 10.9 g
Protein 0.6g
Fiber 0.2g

Creamy Orange Bites

Serves 14

Ingredients
1/2 cup heavy whipping cream
1/2 cup cream cheese
1/2 cup coconut oil, melted
1 tsp. pure orange extract
10 drops Liquid Stevia (or the natural sweetener of your choice)

Directions
1. In an immersion blender place all Ingredients. Blend until corporate well.
2. Add in orange extract and liquid Stevia and mix together with a spoon.
3. Spread the batter mixture into a silicone tray, or in paper muffins trays.
4. Refrigerate for 2 hours. Before serving remove from silicone tray and serve. Keep refrigerated.

Nutritional Facts
Calories 127
Net Carbs 0,3g
Fats 14g
Protein 1g
Fiber 0.01g

Pecan Almond Shortbread Cookies

Makes 20

Ingredients
Pecans (2 cups)
Butter (1 cup, melted)
Vanilla (1 teaspoon)
Almonds (1 cup)
Swerve (3 tablespoons)

Directions
1. Set oven to 325 ℉.
2. Place pecans and almonds in a processor and pulse until fine like flour.
3. Add remaining Ingredients to mixture in processor and mix together until dough is formed.
4. Roll dough into a log and place in fridge for 2 hours or more until dough is set firm.
5. Slice into cookies and place on a lined baking sheet.
6. Bake for 10 minutes.
7. Remove from oven, cool and serve.

Nutritional Facts
Calories 194
Net Carbs 1.2g
Fats 20g
Protein 2.4g
Fiber 1.6g

Butter Pecan Sandwiches

Serves: 2

Ingredients
8 pecan halves
1 Tbsp. unsalted butter, softened
2 oz neufchâtel cheese
1 tsp. orange zest, finely grated
pinch of sea salt

Directions
1. Toast the pecans at 350 degrees Fahrenheit for 5-10 minutes, check often to prevent burning.
2. Mix the butter, neufchâtel cheese, and orange zest until smooth and creamy.
3. Spread the butter mixture between the cooled pecan halves and sandwich together.
4. Sprinkle with sea salt and enjoy!

Nutritional Facts
Calories 243
Net Carbs 1.4g
Fats 26g
Protein 3g
Fiber 1.5g

Lemon Meringue Tarts

Makes 2 (Serves 4)

Ingredients
For curd:
Egg yolks (3)
Liquid stevia (10 drops)
Butter (1/4 cup)
Lemons (2)
Erythritol (1/4 cup, powdered)
Xanthan gum (1 pinch)

For crust:
Whey protein (2 tablespoons)

Egg (1/2)

Salt (1/4 teaspoon)

Almond flour (1cup)

Erythritol (2 tablespoons, powdered)

Butter (1 tablespoon, melted)

For meringue:
Erythritol (2 tablespoons)

Cream of tartar (1/8 teaspoon)

Egg whites (2)

Directions
1. Set oven to 350°F.
2. Prepare crust by mixing all Ingredients together then use hands to knead into a ball.
3. Press crust into tartlet pans and bake for 15 minutes.
4. Start preparing curd as crust bakes by zesting lemons and squeezing juice into a bowl.
5. Combine erythritol, stevia and egg yolks in a metal bowl. Heat water in a pot and place bowl on top of pot and whisk mixture

until it thickens.
6. Add zest and lemon juice then add gum and whisk to thicken mixture.
7. Add butter a little at a time and whisk to combine. Place curd into refrigerator until needed.
8. Prepare meringue by beating whites until foamy then add tartar and beat mixture. Add erythritol little at a time until stiff peaks form.
9. Fill crusts with curd then with meringue and bake for 10 minutes until golden.
10. Cool and serve.

Nutritional Facts
Calories 332
Net Carbs 6g
Fats 29g
Protein 12g
Fiber 3g

Coconut Ginger Squares

Serves 10

Ingredients
1 tsp. dried (powdered) ginger
0.8 oz shredded coconut (unsweetened)
1/3 cup coconut oil, softened
1/3 cup coconut butter, softened
1 tsp. granulated sweetener of choice, to taste

Directions
1. In a deep bowl, mix shredded coconut, coconut oil, coconut butter, sweetener and dried powdered ginger.
2. Pour the ginger mixture into ice block trays and refrigerate for 1 hour to solidify.

Nutritional Facts
Calories 134
Net Carbs 0.3g
Fats 14.5g
Protein 11g
Fiber 0.25g

Spiced Pumpkin Crème Brulee

Serves 2

Ingredients
Heavy cream (1 cup)
Egg yolks (2)
Pumpkin puree (2 tablespoons)
Pumpkin spice (1 teaspoon)
Erythritol (2 tablespoons+2 teaspoons)

Directions
1. Set oven to 300°F.
2. Heat cream in a pan and bring to a boil then remove from heat and add pumpkin spice. Stir and put aside for 5 minutes.
3. Whisk egg yolks then add cream a little at a time and whisk to combine.
4. Add pumpkin puree and continue to whisk mixture together.
5. Add erythritol to mixture and stir together.
6. Place an inch of water into a baking dish and put ramekins into dish. Fill ramekins with crème brulee and bake for 40 minutes. Finished products will be slightly jiggly.
7. Cool for 15 minutes then put into fridge for 4 hours or more.
8. Sprinkle with erythritol and broil for 2 minutes to caramelize the tops of crème brulee.
9. Serve.

Nutritional Facts
Calories 460
Net Carbs 5g
Fats 49g
Protein 5g
Fiber 2.5g

Almond Butter Bombs

Ingredients
2 1/2 cup almond butter
1/2 cup shredded coconut (unsweetened)
2 eggs
1/2 cup Stevia sweetener
1 Tbsp. pure vanilla extract

Directions
1. Preheat oven to 320 F. Line square baking tray with baking paper.
2. Place all Ingredients in a bowl. Knead the mixture by your hands.
3. After the Ingredients are mixed, roll into heaped teaspoon sized balls and place into a baking tray.
4. Bake in the oven for 12 minutes or until the tops of the cookies are browning. Let cool on a wire rack.
5. Serve.

Servings: 24
Cooking Times
Total Time: 22 minutes

Nutrition Facts (per serving)
Carbs: 5,6g
Fiber: 1,8g
Net Carbs: 2,6g
Protein: 7,3g
Fat: 14,5g
Calories: 171

Hazelnut Morsels

Ingredients
1/2 cup ground hazelnuts
1/4 cup hazelnut butter
1 cup cream cheese
1/4 cup cocoa powder
2 Tbsp. Sugar free Hazelnut syrup
Natural sweetener of your cheese, to taste

Directions
1. In a large bowl, place the softened cream cheese (on room temperature) and hazelnut butter. Add in all other Ingredients (except the ground hazelnuts).
2. With a wooden spoon to blend the cream cheese, cocoa powder, butter, syrup and sweetener.
3. In a bowl place the ground hazelnuts. Roll the cream cheese mixture into 16 balls. Dip each ball into the ground hazelnuts.
4. Refrigerate for at least 2-3 hours.

Servings: 16
Cooking Times
Total Time: 15 minutes

Nutrition Facts (per serving)
Carbs: 3,4g
Fiber: 1,4g
Net Carbs: 1,2g
Protein: 3,2g
Fat: 11,6g
Calories: 122

Choco Mint Hazelnut Sticks

Ingredients
4 Tbsp. cocoa powder
1 cup shredded coconut
1 cup hazelnuts
1 tsp. peppermint extract
6 Tbsp. coconut oil, melted
4 Tbsp. almond butter
3/4 cup Stevia sweetener (or some other natural sweetener of your choice)
1 tsp. vanilla extract
pinch of salt

Directions
1. In a large bowl stir together the coconut oil, cacao powder, almond butter, sweetener, vanilla, peppermint extract and salt. Chop the hazelnuts in a food processor.
2. Heat the mixture slowly on low heat over simmering water (double boiler) for 5 to 10 minutes until all Ingredients are combined well.
3. Add hazelnuts and shredded coconut to the melted chocolate mixture and stir together.
4. Pour in a dish lined with parchment and freeze until chocolate is set then cut into sticks.

Servings: 12
Cooking Times
Total Time: 20 minutes

Nutrition Facts (per serving)
Carbs: 5,6g
Fiber: 2,4g
Net Carbs: 2g
Protein: 3g
Fat: 17g
Calories: 174

Chocolate Cookies

Ingredients
1 Tbsp. cacao powder
2 Tbsp. chocolate protein powder
4 Tbsp. coconut milk
2 Tbsp. coconut flour
2 Tbsp. coconut, shredded
1 Tbsp. cacao nibs

Topping:
1 tsp. coconut oil, softened
2/3 cup coconut butter, softened

Directions
1. In a bowl combine all Ingredients (except Ingredients for coating). Whisk 2-3 minutes until well combined.
2. Spoon out mixture into small molds.
3. Place molds in refrigerator for 30 minutes.
4. In a meanwhile prepare coating. In a bowl, mix coconut oil with coconut butter. Remove molds from refrigerator and cover with coating
5. Place back to refrigerator until coating has hardened, about 1 hour.

Servings: 10
Cooking Times
Total Time: 10 minutes

Nutrition Facts (per serving)
Carbs: 2,55g
Fiber: 1g
Net Carbs: 0,71g
Protein: 1g
Fat: 14,47g
Calories: 138

Chocolate Almond Butter Balls

Ingredients
1/2 stick butter, softened
1/2 cup natural peanut butter
2 Tbsp. coconut flour
2 Tbsp. vanilla whey protein powder
1/2 cup broken up sugar free chocolate bars, melted
1 tsp. organic vanilla extract
1 1/2 cup powdered Xylitol (or some other natural sweetener)

Directions
1. In a bowl, mix Almond butter and butter. Beat the butter with an electric hand mixer, beat together butter until smooth.
2. Add in vanilla extract and protein powder to Almond butter mixture, and then mix well.
3. Add in powdered Xylitol sweetener and mix well.
4. On a working surface, roll the dough into 24 two-bite sized balls. Place balls on a pan lined with a parchment paper.
5. Sprinkle each ball with chocolate. Refrigerate for at least 2 hours.

Servings: 12
Cooking Times
Total Time: 10 minutes

Nutrition Facts (per serving)
Carbs: 5,16g
Fiber: 1,02g
Net Carbs: 2,54g
Protein: 3g
Fat: 12g
Calories: 126

Choc-Orange Walnut Muffin

Ingredients
1 1/2 cup walnuts, chopped
4.40 oz dark chocolate, 100% cocoa
1 tsp. natural orange extract
1 tsp. fresh orange peel
4 Tbsp. extra virgin coconut oil
15-20 drops of liquid Stevia
1 tsp. cinnamon

Directions
1. In a heated container of water (water bath) melt the chocolate stirring slightly. Add liquid Stevia, coconut oil and cinnamon. Mix well.
2. Add fresh orange peel and natural orange extract. Add chopped walnuts and mix in well.
3. When ready, with teaspoon place the mixture into small paper muffin.
4. Place in the fridge until solid, at least 4-6 hours.

Servings: 18
Cooking Times
Total Time: 20 minutes

Nutrition Facts (per serving)
Carbs: 5g
Fiber: 1,5g
Net Carbs: 3g
Protein: 13g
Fat: 13g
Calories: 131

Cinnamon Storms

Ingredients
1 cup coconut milk
1 cup almond butter
1 tsp. pure vanilla extract
3/4 tsp. cinnamon
1/2 tsp. nutmeg
1 tsp. natural sweetener to your taste)
1 cup coconut shreds

Directions
1. In a double boiler over medium heat place all the Ingredients (except shredded coconut). Stir all the time to melt and combine well.
2. When ready, remove from the heat. Let cool for 5-6 minutes. Place the bowl in the fridge about 45 minutes until hard.
3. In a bowl put the coconut shreds. Roll the coconut-cinnamon mixture into one inch balls and roll them through the coconut shreds.
4. Place the balls on a serving plate and refrigerate for 2-3 hours.

Servings: 12
Cooking Times
Directions Time: 1 hour and 30 minutes

Nutrition Facts (per serving)
Carbs: 1,6g
Fiber: 0,5g
Net Carbs: 0,2g
Protein: 1g
Fat: 20g
Calories: 184

Creamy Orange Bites

Ingredients
1/2 cup heavy whipping cream
1/2 cup cream cheese
1/2 cup coconut oil, melted
1 tsp. pure orange extract
10 drops Liquid Stevia (or the natural sweetener of your choice)

Directions
1. In an immersion blender place all Ingredients. Blend until corporate well.
2. Add in orange extract and liquid Stevia and mix together with a spoon.
3. Spread the batter mixture into a silicone tray, or in paper muffins trays.
4. Refrigerate for 2 hours. Before serving remove from silicone tray and serve. Keep refrigerated.

Servings: 14
Cooking Times
Total Time: 10 minutes

Nutrition Facts (per serving)
Carbs: 0,5g
Fiber: 0g
Net Carbs: 0,3g
Protein: 1g
Fat: 14g
Calories: 127

Coco-Nut Bombs

Ingredients
1 1/2 cup flaked coconut, unsweetened
1 cup coconut oil
1 cup extra virgin coconut oil
1 tsp. cinnamon powder
1/8 tsp. salt
2 Tbsp. of powdered Erythritol

Directions
1. Preheat the oven 350 F.
2. Arrange evenly the flaked coconut on a rectangular baking tray. Place in the oven and toast for 8 minutes strictly. Let cool 2-3 minutes.
3. Transfer baked coconut into a blender and pulse until get a smooth and runny consistency.
4. Add the softened coconut oil, vanilla, Erythritol, salt and cinnamon. Blend well.
5. Pour the mixture with the tablespoon into ice cube tray to get 12 servings. Refrigerate for at least 2-3 hours.
6. Ready. Serve and enjoy! Keep refrigerated.

Servings: 12
Cooking Times
Total Time: 15 minutes

Nutrition Facts (per serving)
Carbs: 1,5g
Fiber: 1g
Net Carbs: 0,6g
Protein: 0,4g
Fat: 13g
Calories: 114

Easy Choc Blueberry Squares

Ingredients
5 Tbsp. butter
3 Tbsp. coconut oil
2 Tbsp. sugar-free Blueberry syrup
2 Tbsp. cocoa powder

Directions
1. In a sauce pan add all Ingredients and cook over low heat until chocolate sauce texture.
2. Pour into mold and freeze for at least 3 hours.
3. Before serving unmold and enjoy.

Servings: 6
Cooking Times
Total Time: 15 minutes

Nutrition Facts (per serving)
Carbs: 1g
Fiber: 0,6g
Net Carbs: 0,05
Protein: 0,5g
Fat: 17g
Calories: 148

Lemon Coconut Balls

Ingredients
1/4 cup shredded coconut, unsweetened,
1 cup cream cheese
1 Tbsp. pure lemon extract
Natural sweetener of your choice, to taste
1/4 cup butter

Directions
1. In a bowl, combine cream cheese, natural sweetener and lemon extract. Blend all Ingredients together well with mixing spoon. Place bowl in refrigerator for 15-20 minutes.
2. In a bowl place unsweetened shredded coconut. Roll lemon batter into 16 equal balls.
3. Dip each ball into coconut and place on a serving pan. Refrigerate for 3-4 hours at least. Serve.

Servings: 12
Cooking Times
Directions Time: 15 minutes

Nutrition Facts (per serving)
Carbs: 1g
Fiber: 0,2g
Net Carbs: 0,8g
Protein: 1,3g
Fat: 12g
Calories: 106

Gingery Coconut Bomb

Ingredients
1 tsp. dried (powdered) ginger
0.8 oz shredded coconut (unsweetened)
1/3 cup coconut oil, softened
1/3 cup coconut butter, softened
1 tsp. granulated sweetener of choice, to taste

Directions
1. In a deep bowl, mix shredded coconut, coconut oil, coconut butter, sweetener and dried powdered ginger.
2. Pour the ginger mixture into ice block trays and refrigerate for 1 hour to solidify.

Servings: 10
Cooking Times
Total Time: 5 minutes

Nutrition Facts (per serving)
Carbs: 2,5g
Fiber: 0,25g
Net Carbs: 0,3g
Protein:
Fat: 14,5g
Calories: 134

Homemade Almond Butter

Ingredients
3 cups almonds (no salt added)
1 tsp. Himalayan salt
1 tsp. cinnamon
1 vanilla pod or bean, halved and seeds removed
2 Tbsp. Stevia powder or Erythritol sweetener

Directions
1. Preheat oven to 360F degrees. Place almonds in a baking pan and bake for 10-12 minutes. Stir occasionally to not burn.
2. Transfer the almonds in a food processor and add remaining Ingredients.
3. Process for 15 minutes above. This process takes a time so, you have to be patient. Pour the almond butter to a glass container and store in the refrigerator.

Servings: 14
Cooking Times
Total Time: 40 minutes

Nutrition Facts (per serving)
Carbs: 5,5g
Fiber: 2,8g
Net Carbs: 1.3g
Protein: 5g
Fat: 13,5g
Calories: 153g

Almond Cookies Bombs

Ingredients
1 cup almonds, chopped
1 cup butter, softened
2 1/4 cups almond flour
1 1/4 cup cocoa powder
3 1/2 Tbsp. coconut flour
2 eggs
3/4 cup Stevia powder
2 tsp. vanilla extract
1/2 tsp. baking soda
1/4 tsp. sea salt

Directions
1. Preheat oven to 340F degrees.
2. In a bowl, whisk butter and sweetener. Add the eggs, coconut oil and vanilla extract.
3. In a separate bowl, mix together the baking soda, almond flour, coconut flour, cocoa powder and salt.
4. Combine the eggs mixture to the flour mixture. Pour dough in a greased baking pan. Sprinkle dough with chopped almond over top.
5. Bake for 15-18 minutes. Let cool and cut into chunks. Serve.

Servings: 16
Cooking Times
Total Time: 25 minutes

Nutrition Facts (per serving)
Carbs: 3,35g
Fiber: 1g
Net Carbs: 0,5g
Protein: 2,9g
Fat: 17g
Calories: 171

Hazelnut Squares

Ingredients
1/2 cup hazelnuts, chopped
1 cup whipped cream
1/4 cup cocoa butter
2 Tbsp. cocoa powder, unsweetened
2 Tbsp. Stevia sweetener
Crushed walnuts (optional extra)

Directions
1. In a bowl, melt cocoa butter at room temperature.
2. When ready, add in cocoa powder, Stevia powder and mix well until all Ingredients are well blended. Add in chopped hazelnuts and stir well.
3. Finally, add whipping cream and mix well.
4. Pour the hazelnut mixture in squared molds and let cool. (ice trays work just fine)
5. Refrigerate for 1 - 2 hours. Dress with crushed walnuts if so desired Serve.

Servings: 6
Cooking Times
Total Time: 15 minutes

Nutrition Facts (per serving)
Carbs: 3,8g
Fiber: 1,3g
Net Carbs: 0,5g
Protein: 2g
Fat: 16,5g
Calories: 160

Lime Mini Muffins

Ingredients
fresh lime zest from 2 organic limes
1 cup extra virgin coconut oil, softened
3/4 cup coconut butter, softened
20 drops Erythritol extract (or some other natural sweetener of your choice)
pinch of salt

Directions
1. Soft the coconut butter and coconut oil on room temperature.
2. Zest the organic limes.
3. In a bowl mix all the Ingredients in a bowl and stir well. Make sure that lime zest and Erythritol extract are distributed evenly.
4. Prepare 16 mini muffin cups.
5. Refrigerate for 2 hours. Ready. Keep refrigerated.

Servings: 16
Cooking Times
Total Time: 10 minutes

Nutrition Facts (per serving)
Carbs: 0,9g
Fiber: 0,3g
Net Carbs: 0,15g
Protein: 0,2g
Fat: 12,5g
Calories: 109

Lemony Cream Cheese Bombshells

Ingredients
1/2 cup butter, unsalted and softened
1 cup cream cheese, softened
1/2 tsp. pure lemon extract
3/4 cup granular Stevia

Directions
1. Place all Ingredients in a deep bowl. Beat the mixture with an electric mixer several minutes, until soft.
2. When ready, place cream cheese mixture by teaspoon size, one by one onto a wax paper-lined sheet.
3. Freeze until firm, at least 2 hours. Remove to freezer and serve frozen.

Servings: 12

Cooking Times
Total Time: 2 hours

Nutrition Facts (per serving)
Carbs: 0,8g
Fiber: 0g
Net Carbs: 0,7g
Protein: 1,3g
Fat: 14.5g
Calories: 134

Heavenly Lemon Quads with Coconut Cream

Ingredients
Base
3/4 cup coconut flakes
2 Tbsp. coconut oil
1 Tbsp. ground almonds
Cream
5 eggs
1/2 lemon juice
1 Tbsp. coconut flour
1/2 cup Stevia sweetener

Directions
Base
1. Preheat oven to 360F.
2. In a bowl put all base Ingredients and with clean hands mix everything well until soft.
3. With coconut oil grease a rectangle oven dish. Pour dough in a baking pan. Bake for 15 minutes until golden brown. Set aside to cool.

Cream
1. In a bowl or blender, whisk together: eggs, lemon juice, coconut flour and sweetener. Pour over the baked caked evenly.
2. Put pan in the oven and bake 20 minutes more.
3. When ready refrigerate for at least 6 hours. Cut in cubes & serve.

Servings: 8

Cooking Times
Total Time: 1 hour and 5 minutes

Nutrition Facts (per serving)
Carbs: 4g
Fiber: 2,25g
Net Carbs: 1,4g
Protein: 5g
Fat: 15g
Calories: 129

Macadamia Cacao bites

Ingredients
1 cup macadamia nuts, chopped
1/2 cup cacao powder
2 cups almond flour
1/2 cup ground flax
3 Tbsp. coconut oil (melted)
1/3 cup Stevia or natural sweetener of your choice
1/3 cup water
1/2 tsp. pure vanilla extract

Directions
1. In a bowl, mix almond flour and flax and cacao powder. Stir in oil, water, sweetener and vanilla. When it is well mixed, stir in chopped hazelnuts.
2. Form the mixture into balls, press flat with palms and place on dehydrator screens.
3. Dehydrate 1 hour at 145, then reduce to 116 and dehydrate for at least 5 hours or until desired dryness is achieved.

Servings: 24

Cooking Times
Total Time: 6 hours

Nutrition Facts (per serving)
Carbs: 7g
Fiber: 3g
Net Carbs: 3,4
Protein: 3,5g
Fat: 13g
Calories: 143

Minty Galettes

Ingredients

3 cup coconut butter, melted
1 cup coconut, shredded
3 Tbsp. coconut oil melted
3/4 tsp. pure peppermint extract
2 Tbsp. cacao powder

Directions

1. In a bowl, mix together, 1 tablespoon of coconut oil and peppermint extract, shredded coconut and melted coconut butter.
2. Pour coconut butter mixture into mini muffin tins by filling half way. Put in refrigerator for about 20 minutes.
3. In a separate bowl mix together 2 tablespoons coconut oil and cacao powder.
4. After 20 minutes remove muffin tin from refrigerator and pour each with cacao mixture.
5. Return to refrigerator for 3-4 hours. Ready!

Servings: 18

Cooking Times
Total Time: 20 minutes
Nutrition Facts (per serving)

Nutrition Facts (per serving)
Carbs: 0,5g
Fiber: 0,3g
Net Carbs: 0,1g
Protein: 0,25g
Fat: 11g
Calories: 93

Almond Butter Cake with Chocolate Sauce

Ingredients
1 cup peanut butter
1/4 cup almond milk, unsweetened
1 cup coconut oil
2 tsp. liquid Stevia sweetener to taste
Topping: Chocolate Sauce
2 Tbsp. coconut oil, melted
4 Tbsp. cocoa powder, unsweetened
2 Tbsp. Stevia sweetener

Directions
1. In a microwave bowl mix coconut oil and peanut butter; melt in a microwave for 1-2 minutes.
2. Add this mixture to your blender; add in the rest of the Ingredients and blend well until combined.
3. Pour the peanut mixture into a parchment lined loaf pan or platter.
4. Refrigerate for about 3 hours; the longer, the better.
5. In a bowl, whisk all topping Ingredients together. Pour over the peanut candy after it's been set. Cut into cubes and serve.

Servings: 12

Cooking Times
Total Time: 5 minutes

Nutrition Facts (per serving)
Carbs: 5,8g
Fiber: 2g
Net Carbs: 2,4g
Protein: 6g
Fat: 27g
Calories: 273

Peppermint Coconut Bombs

Ingredients

1 1/4 cup seed butter
1 tsp. peppermint extract
1 1/2 cups coconut oil
1/2 cup sweetener (liquid or granulated)
2 tsp. organic vanilla extract
1/4 tsp. salt

Directions
1. First, in a small saucepan melt the coconut oil.
2. In a blender add all remaining Ingredients and add melted coconut oil. Blend it until smooth well.
3. With the teaspoon grab the coconut mixture and make the 25 coconut balls.
4. Place the balls into a baking sheet and freeze until solid. Keep refrigerated.

Servings: 25

Cooking Times
Total Time: 10 minutes

Nutrition Facts (per serving)
Carbs: 8g
Fiber: 1.2g
Net Carbs: 0,25g
Protein: 2.25g
Fat: 19g
Calories: 202

Pistachio Masala Bombs

Ingredients
1 cup almond butter, melted
1/4 cup ghee
1 cup coconut oil
1/2 cup cocoa butter
1/4 cup pistachio nuts
1 Tbsp. coconut milk
1 Tbsp. pure vanilla extract
2 tsp. Masala chai (a flavored tea beverage made by brewing black tea with a mixture of aromatic Indian spices and herbs)

Directions
1. In a small saucepan melt the cocoa butter over LOW heat.
2. In a large bowl add all Ingredients (except the cocoa butter and pistachios).
3. Use a hand mixer and mix well (on HIGH) all Ingredients until the mixture combine evenly. Add in the melted butter and continue to blend for 1-2 minutes more.
4. Transfer the mixture to greased and paper lined pan. Sprinkle with chopped pistachios and refrigerate for at least 5 hours.

Servings: 32

Cooking Times
Total Time: 15 minutes

Nutrition Facts (per serving)
Carbs: 0,4g
Fiber: 0,1g
Net Carbs: 0,1g
Protein: 0,27
Fat: 17g
Calories: 147

Raspberry Heaven Bombs

Ingredients
3 Tbsp. heavy cream
1/4 cup coconut oil, melted
8 oz. cream cheese, softened
1/4 cup coconut oil, melted
3 tsp. raspberry extract
1/2 cup powdered Erythritol
pinch salt
few drops of natural red food coloring

Directions
1. Prepare the parchment lined baking sheet.
2. In a bowl, with the hand mixer, blend the cream cheese and sweetener together.
3. Add the raspberry extract, natural food coloring cream, salt and raspberry extract and continue to blend.
4. Add in the coconut oil and continue to blend until it's smooth and creamy.
5. Refrigerate this mixture for 1 hour.
6. When ready, make 48 small balls from batter and place into a prepared parchment lined baking sheet. Place it in a freezer for 2 hours.

Servings: 18

Cooking Times
Total Time: 15 minutes

Nutrition Facts (per serving)
Carbs: 0,6g
Fiber: 0g
Net Carbs: 0.4g
Protein: 0,77
Fat: 12g
Calories: 101

Simple Coconut Treats

Ingredients
1 Tbsp. shredded coconut
1/3 cup coconut oil, melted
1/3 cup coconut butter, softened
1 tsp. granulated sweetener of choice, to taste

Directions
1. Prepare the ice cube trays.
2. Mix all the Ingredients in a deep bowl until your natural sweetener is dissolved.
3. Pour batter into ice cube trays.
4. Place in refrigerator for 30 minutes. Enjoy!

Servings: 10

Cooking Times
Total Time: 5 minutes

Nutrition Facts (per serving)
Carbs: 2,4g
Fiber: 0,1g
Net Carbs: 0,3g
Protein: 0,2g
Fat: 14g
Calories: 129

Slow Cooker Pecan Nuts

Ingredients

2 cups Pecans nuts, halves
4 Tbsp. almond butter
1 cup Stevia or any other natural sweetener
1/4 tsp. ground ginger
1/4 tsp. ground allspice
1 1/2 tsp. ground cinnamon

Directions
1. In a 4-quart Slow Cooker stir the Pecans nuts halves and almond butter until combined.
2. Add Stevia or any natural sweetener of your choice and stir well.
3. Transfer to a bowl, combine spices and sprinkle over nuts.
4. Cover and cook on HIGH for 15 minutes. Turn to LOW and cook uncovered for about 2 hours, or until the nuts are a little crispy.

Servings: 8
Cooking Times
Total Time: 2 hours and 15 minutes

Nutrition Facts (per serving)
Carbs: 3,6g
Fiber: 2,3g
Net Carbs: 0,88g
Protein: 2,9g
Fat: 14g
Calories: 140

Strawberry Cream-cakes

Ingredients
5 strawberries
1/2 cup heavy cream
5 Tbsp. butter
5 Tbsp. coconut oil
3 Tbsp. Truvia (or any favorite sweetener)
1 peace dark 100%, sugar free chocolate

Directions
1. In a bowl, mix heavy cream and the strawberries.
2. With a help of an immersion blender, blend together heavy cream and strawberries.
3. In a separate bowl, add granulated sweetener and the butter; melt butter mixture in the microwave about 30 seconds.
4. Add the butter mixture to a heavy cream and strawberries and blend well.
5. Spoon mixture into your favorite molds. Freeze at least 30 minutes; the longer, the better.
6. Remove mixture from the mold, place on wax paper and melt one piece sugar free chocolate.
7. Pour melted chocolate over the cream and return to freezer for another 30 minutes.

Servings: 12

Cooking Times
Total Time: 1 hour and 10 minutes

Nutrition Facts (per serving)
Carbs: 0,6g
Fiber: 0,08g
Net Carbs: 0,2g
Protein: 0,3gr
Fat: 16g
Calories: 138

Creamy Strawberry Muffins

Ingredients
3/4 cup cream cheese, softened
1/4 cup butter, softened
1/2 cup strawberries, fresh or frozen
1 Tbsp. pure vanilla extract
10-15 drops liquid Stevia

Directions
1. In a mixing bowl, place the butter and the cream cheese and eave at room temperature (about 45min) until softened. Do not microwave the butter!
2. In a separate bowl place the strawberries and mash using a fork.
3. Add the liquid Stevia and vanilla extract and mix well. Add the strawberries to the bowl with softened butter and cream cheese. Whisk until all Ingredients are well combined.
4. Pour the strawberry mixture into muffin silicon molds. Place in the freezer for about 3-4 hours.
5. Before serving, unmold the strawberry muffins and place on a serving dish. Keep refrigerated.

Servings: 10

Cooking Times
Total Time: 10 minutes

Nutrition Facts (per serving)
Carbs: 1,5g
Fiber: 0,2g
Net Carbs: 1,1g
Protein: 1,15g
Fat: 11g
Calories: 107

Walnuts Choc Squares

Ingredients

1/3 cup heavy cream
1/2 cup cocoa butter
1/2 cup pecans, roughly chopped
1/2 cup coconut oil
4 Tbsp. cocoa powder, unsweetened
4 Tbsp. Swerve, Stevia or Erythritol sweetener

Directions

1. In a microwave dish, place cocoa butter and coconut oil together. Use the defrost setting on your microwave and melt in microwave stove for 10-15 seconds.
2. Add in cocoa powder and whisk well. Pour mixture into a blender with sweetener and cream and blend for 3-4 minutes.
3. Place silicone molds onto a sheet pan and fill halfway with walnuts.
4. Pour the mixture with walnuts and place in refrigerator for 6 hours.

Servings: 10

Cooking Times
Total Time: 10 minutes

Nutrition Facts (per serving)
Carbs: 2,23g
Fiber: 1,25g
Net Carbs:0,25g
Protein: 1g
Fat: 29g
Calories: 150

Almond Butter Cake with Choco Sauce

Ingredients
1 cup almond butter or soaked almonds
1/4 cup almond milk, unsweetened
1 cup coconut oil
2 tsp. liquid Stevia sweetener to taste
Topping: Chocolate Sauce
4 Tbsp. cocoa powder, unsweetened
2 Tbsp. almond butter
2 Tbsp. Stevia sweetener

Directions
1. Melt the coconut oil in room temperature.
2. Add all Ingredients in a bowl and blend well until combined.
3. Pour the almond butter mixture into a parchment lined platter.
4. Place in refrigerator for 3 hours.
5. In a bowl, whisk all topping Ingredients together. Pour over the almond cake after it's been set.
6. Cut into cubes and serve.

Servings: 12

Cooking Times
Total Time: 5 minutes

Nutrition Facts (per serving)
Carbs: 9,8g
Fiber: 2g
Net Carbs: 2,4g
Protein: 5,8g
Fat: 23,3g
Calories: 273

Butter Pecan Biscuits

Ingredients
8 pecan halves
1 Tbsp. unsalted butter, softened
2 oz neufchâtel cheese
1 tsp. orange zest, finely grated
pinch of sea salt

Directions
1. Toast the pecans at 350 degrees Fahrenheit for 5-10 minutes, check often to prevent burning.
2. Mix the butter, neufchâtel cheese, and orange zest until smooth and creamy.
3. Spread the butter mixture between the cooled pecan halves and sandwich together.
4. Sprinkle with sea salt and enjoy!

Servings: 2

Nutrition Facts (per serving)
Carbs: 3,31g
Fiber: 1,5g
Net Carbs: 1,4g
Protein: 3g
Fat: 26g
Calories: 243

Author Notes
Pecans contain more than 19 vitamins and minerals and are also rich in age defying antioxidants. They're rich in fiber which boosts the health of your heart and phenolic antioxidants that help to prevent coronary artery disease.

Choco Almond Bombs

Ingredients
3 Tbsp. cocoa powder, unsweetened
1 cup almond butter
1 cup organic coconut oil
3-4 Tbsp. sweetener to taste
Splash of almond extract (optional)

Directions
1. In a saucepan over medium heat, melt coconut oil and almond butter. Stir in cocoa powder and sweetener of your choice. Remove from heat and add almond extract.
2. Pour almond mixture into silicone candy molds. Freeze or refrigerate until set.
3. Before using remove from molds and store in a fridge in an air tight container.

Servings: 24

Cooking Times
Total Time: 10 minutes

Nutrition Facts (per serving)
Carbs: 0,4g
Fiber: 1,22g
Net Carbs: 0g
Protein: 0,5g
Fat: 9,6g
Calories: 75

Chocolate-Coconut Layered Cups

Ingredients
Bottom Layer:
1/2 cup coconut butter
1/2 cup coconut oil
1/2 cup unsweetened, shredded coconut
3 Tbsp. powdered sweetener such as Splenda or Truvia

Top Layer:
1/2 cup cocoa butter
1 oz unsweetened chocolate
1/4 cup powdered sweetener such as Splenda or Truvia
1/4 cup cocoa powder
1/2 tsp. vanilla extract

Directions
1. Prepare a mini-muffin pan with 20 mini paper liners.

For the bottom layer:
1. Combine coconut butter and coconut oil in a small saucepan over low heat. Stir until smooth and melted then add the shredded coconut and powdered sweetener until combined.
2. Divide the mixture among prepared mini muffin cups and freeze until firm, about 30 minutes.

For the top layer:
1. Combine cocoa butter and unsweetened chocolate together in double boiler or a bowl set over a pan of simmering water. Stir until melted.
2. Stir in the powdered sweetener, then the cocoa powder and mix until smooth.
3. Remove from heat and stir in the vanilla extract.
4. Spoon chocolate topping over chilled coconut candies and let set, about 15 minutes.
5. Enjoy!

Servings: 10

Nutrition Facts (per serving)
Carbs: 2,7g
Fiber: 1,5g
Net Carbs: 0,35g
Protein: 1g
Fat: 27,5g
Calories: 247

Author Notes
Chocolate contains antioxidants known as polyphenols. Polyphenols play an important role in the prevention of degenerative diseases such as cancer and cardiovascular diseases.

Chocolate-Walnut Bites

Ingredients
1/2 cup coconut oil
1 oz cocoa powder
1 Tbsp. sugar substitute
1 oz walnut pieces
1 Tbsp. tahini paste
Walnut halves for topping the Fatbombs

Directions
1. Warm the coconut oil in the microwave until melted.
2. Add the remaining Ingredients and stir until well combined.
3. Pour into silicone ice cube trays and refrigerate until almost set.
4. Once almost set, add walnut halves to the top of each Fatbomb.
5. Return to fridge until firm.
6. Remove from silicone molds and store in an airtight container in the fridge for up to a week.

Servings: 14

Nutrition Facts (per serving)
Carbs: 2,5g
Dietary Fiber:1g
Net Carbs: 1g
Protein: 0,7g
Fat: 10g
Calories: 88,5

Author Notes
Walnuts have been touted as one of the world's most healthiest foods. Research shows that walnut consumption may support brain health and improve cell function. They contain a good amount of healthy omega-3 fats and are delicious to boot!

Cinnamon Bun Bombs

Ingredients
1 cup coconut butter
1 cup full Fatcoconut milk (from a can)
1 cup unsweetened coconut shreds
1 tsp. vanilla extract
1/2 tsp. cinnamon
1/2 tsp. nutmeg
1 tsp. sugar substitute such as Splenda

Directions
1. Combine all Ingredients except the shredded coconut together in double boiler or a bowl set over a pan of simmering water. Stir until everything is melted and combined.
2. Remove bowl from heat and place in the fridge until the mixture has firmed up and can be rolled into balls.
3. Form the mixture into 1" balls, a small cookie scoop is helpful for doing this.
4. Roll each ball in the shredded coconut until well coated.
5. Serve and enjoy! Store in the fridge.

Servings: 10

Cooking Times
Total Time: 15 minutes

Nutrition Facts (per serving)
Carbs: 2g
Fiber: 1g
Net Carbs: 0,6g
Protein: 0,7g

Author Notes
Cinnamon is not only delicious, but it's one of the healthiest spices on the planet! It can help to lower blood sugar levels and reduce heart disease risk factors. It's also loaded with powerful antioxidants.

Coconut & Matcha Balls

Ingredients

For the truffles:
1 cup firm coconut oil (refrigerate if necessary)
1 cup coconut butter
1/2 cup full Fatcoconut milk, refrigerated overnight
1/2 tsp. matcha green tea powder
1/4 tsp. cinnamon
1/4 tsp. sea salt
1 tsp. pure vanilla extract

For the truffle coating:
1 cup finely shredded, unsweetened coconut
1 Tbsp. matcha green tea powder

Directions
1. Combine all of the truffle Ingredients in a medium sized mixing bowl. Note that it's very important for your coconut oil be firm so send it to the fridge for a little bit if you have to. Same goes for the coconut milk - the thick cream will rise to the top and coconut water will sink to the bottom. While it's not mandatory that you use only the cream part, your milk should be very firm when you use it so make sure that you cool the can overnight.
2. Mix on high speed with a hand mixer, until light and fluffy, then place in the refrigerator to firm up for about an hour.
3. While the truffle mixture is firming up, combine the shredded coconut and matcha powder together in a large, shallow dish. Set aside.
4. With the help of a small cookie scoop form the cold truffle mixture into 32 little balls, roughly the size of a ping pong ball.
5. Roll the balls quickly between the palms of your hands to shape them into perfect little spheres, then drop each ball into the coconut/matcha mixture and roll them until completely coated.
6. Transfer your finished balls to an airtight container and keep refrigerated for up to 2 weeks.
7. These can be eaten straight out of the fridge but taste best when you let them sit at room temperature for 10 to 15 minutes before to eat them.

Servings: 32

Nutrition Facts (per serving)
Carbs: 0,6g
Fiber: 0,3g
Net Carbs: 0,2g
Protein: 0,2g
Fat: 14g
Calories: 123

Almond Butter Fudge

Ingredients
1 cup all natural creamy peanut butter
1 cup coconut oil
1/4 cup unsweetened vanilla almond milk
a pinch of coarse sea salt
1 tsp. vanilla extract
2 tsp. liquid stevia (optional)

Directions
1. In a microwave safe bowl, soften the Almond butter and coconut oil together. (About 1 minute on med-low heat.)
2. Combine the softened Almond butter and coconut oil with the remaining Ingredients into a blender or food processor.
3. Blend until thoroughly combined.
4. Pour into a 9X4" loaf pan that has been lined with parchment paper.
5. Refrigerate until set. About 2 hours.
6. Enjoy!

Servings: 12
Cooking Times: 15 minutes

Nutrition Facts (per serving)
Carbs: 4,25g
Fiber: 1,3g
Net Carbs: 2g
Protein: 5,4g
Fat: 29g
Calories: 284

Author Notes
Coconut oil has a multitude of health benefits including improving glucose tolerance and decreasing risk of cardiovascular disease.

Rich & Creamy Ice Cream

Ingredients
4 whole pastured eggs
4 yolks from pastured eggs
1/2 cup melted cocoa butter
1/4 cup melted coconut oil
15-20 drops Liquid Stevia
1/2 cup cocoa powder
1 cup MCT oil
2 tsp. pure vanilla extract
8-10 ice cubes

Directions
1. Add all Ingredients but the ice cubes into the jug of your high speed blender. Blend on high for 2 minutes, until creamy.
2. While the blender is running, remove the top portion of the lid and drop in 1 ice cube at a time, allowing the blender to run about 10 seconds between each ice cube.
3. Once all of the ice has been added, pour the cold mixture into a 9×5" loaf pan and place in the freezer. Set the timer for 30 minutes before taking out to stir. Repeat this process for for 2-3 hours, until desired consistency is met.
4. Serve immediately. Top with chopped nuts or shaved dark chocolate. Store covered in the freezer for up to a week.

Servings: 8
Nutrition Facts (per serving)
Carbs: 2,21g
Fiber: 1,20g
Protein: 0,7g
Fat: 25,4g
Calories: 230

Author Notes
MCTs are medium-chain triglycerides, a form of saturated fatty acid that has numerous health benefits, ranging from improved cognitive function to better weight management. Coconut oil contains about 65% MCTs, but pure MCT oil can be found at many health food stores.

Almond Butter Fudge

Ingredients
1 cup almond butter (unsweetened)
1 cup coconut milk
1 cup coconut oil
1 tsp. vanilla extract
Sweetener of your choice to taste

Directions
1. In a bowl, melt the almond butter and coconut oil.
2. Blend all the Ingredients together well.
3. Pour the mixture into a lined baking pan with parchment paper. Refrigerate for several hours to set.
4. Cut into pieces and serve.

Servings: 12

Cooking Times
Total Time: 5 minutes

Nutrition Facts (per serving)
Carbs: 4,24g
Fiber: 2,15g
Net Carbs: 0,97g
Protein: 4,45g
Fat: 27,4g
Calories: 295,62

Blackberry Coconut Porridge with Pumpkin Seeds

Ingredients
1/4 cup ground flaxseed
1/4 cup coconut flour
1 tsp. pure vanilla extract
1 cup coconut milk
1 tsp. cinnamon
Liquid sweetener of your choice
Toppings
1 cup blackberries (any type)
2 Tbsp. coconut, shaved
2 Tbsp. pumpkin seeds

Directions
1. In a saucepan heat the coconut milk. Add in coconut flour, cinnamon, flaxseed and whisk. Add in vanilla extract and liquid sweetener of your choice.
2. Cook for 10 minutes stirring constantly. Remove from heat and let rest for two-three minutes,
3. Decorate with fresh blackberries, pumpkin seeds and shaved coconut. Serve.

Servings: 4

Cooking Times
Total Time: 5 minutes

Nutrition Facts (per serving)
Carbs: 16,15g
Fiber: 2,07g
Net Carbs: 2,51g
Protein: 0,7g
Fat: 14,15g
Calories: 197

Choc Coffee-Coconut Bombs

Ingredients
3/4 cup coconut butter
2 Tbsp. coconut oil
4 Tbsp. 100% cocoa powder
2 Tbsp. ground coffee
2 Tbsp. coconut flakes, unsweetened
1 tsp. sweetener of your choice, or to taste

Directions
1. In a microwave, melt the coconut butter.
2. Mix in all the Ingredients (except the coconut oil) and mix well with a fork.+
3. Prepare an ice-cube tray.
4. Spoon the mixture into each cup of the ice-cube tray and gently pat them flat with a fork.
5. Freeze for 4-5 hours.
6. Defrost at room temperature for 30 minutes before serving.

Servings: 10

Cooking Times
Total Time: 10 minutes

Nutrition Facts (per serving)
Carbs: 1,57g
Fiber: 0,81g
Net Carbs: 0,25g
Protein: 0,61g
Fat: 19,87g
Calories: 178,54

Delicious Coconut Brownies

Ingredients
3/4 cup organic cocoa
1/2 cup shredded coconut
1/2 cup walnuts, chopped
1/2 cup full Fatcanned coconut milk
2 eggs
1/2 cup Sweetener of your choice
1 cup coconut oil, melted
1 tsp. vanilla extract
1 cup almond flour, heaping
1/2 tsp. baking soda

Directions
1. Preheat the oven to 350 degrees.
2. In a bowl, mix together the coconut oil, coconut milk, vanilla, cocoa, eggs and sweetener.
3. In another bowl combine the shredded coconut, almond flour and baking soda.
4. Combine the two bowls together and pour into a square baking dish.
5. Bake for 30 minutes. Once ready, let cool for 15 before serving. Enjoy!

Servings: 12

Cooking Times
Total Time: 40 minutes

Nutrition Facts (per serving)
Carbs: 8,73g
Fiber: 3,72g
Net Carbs: 2,17g
Protein: 5,29g
Fat: 27,13g
Calories: 278,93

Macadamia Butter Fudge

Ingredients
1 cup macadamia butter
1 cup coconut oil
1/4 cup almond milk, unsweetened
1 tsp. vanilla extract
2 tsp. liquid stevia (optional)
a pinch of coarse sea salt

Directions
1. Combine the macadamia butter and coconut oil with the remaining Ingredients into a blender or food processor.
2. Blend until thoroughly combined.
3. Pour into a 9X4 loaf pan that has been lined with parchment paper.
4. Refrigerate about 2 hours. Serve!

Servings: 12

Cooking Times
Total Time: 15 minutes

Nutrition Facts (per serving)
Carbs: 4,25g
Fiber: 1,29g
Net Carbs: 2,03g
Protein: 5,39g
Fat: 24,4g
Calories: 284,02

Mini Lemony Vanilla Cubes

Ingredients
1 cup extra virgin coconut oil, softened
1 cup coconut butter, softened
1/2 vanilla bean seeds
1 lemon, zest and juice

Directions
1. In a bowl, blend and whisk all Ingredients together.
2. Line a loaf pan with parchment paper. Pour the mixture into the pan, refrigerate for approximately 30 minutes or until firm.
3. Cut into cubes before serving. Decorate with lemon zest. (optional)

Servings: 12

Cooking Times
Total Time: 10 minutes

Nutrition Facts (per serving)
Carbs: 0,35g
Fiber: 0,01g
Net Carbs: 0,13g
Protein: 0,1g
Fat: 16,77g
Calories: 147,2

Minty Fudge

Ingredients
1 cup coconut oil
1 cup organic cocoa powder
1 cup full Fatcoconut milk
1 cup sweetener of your choice
1 tsp. peppermint extract
1 tsp. almond extract
1 tsp. Celtic sea salt

Directions
1. Place a sheet of parchment or wax paper along the inside of a loaf pan and place in the freezer for at least 15 minutes.
2. In a bowl, place the coconut oil and coconut milk a medium and mix with a hand mixer on HIGH speed for 5-6 minutes.
3. Add in remaining Ingredients and stir on LOW speed until the cocoa is combined. Add the sweetener of your choice to taste.
4. Pour the batter in a prepared loaf pan. Refrigerate for several hours.
5. Before serving, use a sharp knife to cut the fudge into squares.
6. Serve.

Servings: 12

Cooking Times
Total Time: 20 minutes

Nutrition Facts (per serving)
Carbs: 4,44g
Fiber: 0,59g
Net Carbs: 2,83g
Protein: 0,51g
Fat: 19,45g
Calories: 183,82

Pumpkin Pie Bombs

Ingredients
1 cup shredded coconut, unsweetened
1 cup coconut oil
3 cup pumpkin puree, unsweetened
1 Tbsp. ground cinnamon
1 1 tsp. ground ginger
1 tsp. pure vanilla extract
25 drops sweetener of your choice, extract
pinch ground cloves
pinch of Himalayan rock salt

Directions
1. Line a baking sheet with two 12-count mini muffin silicon molds.
2. In a your food processor, add shredded coconut, coconut oil, sweetener of your choice and salt. Blend on HIGH speed for 7-8 minutes.
3. Once smooth, remove 1 cup of the coconut mixture, leaving the remaining coconut mix in the food processor bowl. Add remaining Ingredients and process until smooth again.
4. Scoop about 2 teaspoons into each muffin cup. Press down with fingers or the back of a spoon until completely flat. Then, top with reserved white coconut mixture. Transfer baking sheet to the freezer and freeze for 1 hour.

Servings: 12

Cooking Times
Total Time: 1 hour and 20 minutes

Nutrition Facts (per serving)
Carbs: 2,83g
Fiber: 1,39g
Net Carbs: 0,95g
Protein: 0,42g
Fat: 11,37g
Calories: 109,16

Simple Coconut Cream with Berries

Ingredients
1 can (15 oz) full Fatcoconut milk, unsweetened
1/2 cup fresh blueberries
dark chocolate shavings

Directions
1. Store the coconut milk in the fridge overnight.
2. Scoop out the thick part of the coconut milk leaving the water behind.
3. In a bowl, whip with a hand mixer for several minutes.
4. Add in blueberries.
5. Top with chocolate shavings.
6. Serve.

Servings: 4

Cooking Times
Total Time: 10 minutes
Nutrition Facts (per serving)

Carbs: 9,25g
Fiber: 0,94g
Net Carbs: 4,1g
Protein: 1,48g
Fat: 14,93g
Calories: 167,72

Cacao Dream Bonbons

Ingredients
Candies
1/2 cup shredded coconut, unsweetened
1/2 cup coconut butter
1/2 cup coconut oil
3 Tbsp. sweetener of your choice, to taste
Topping
1/4 cup cocoa butter
1/4 cup cocoa powder
3 oz Sugar-free dark chocolate
1/4 cup powdered sweetener of your choice (optional)
1/4 tsp. vanilla extract

Directions
1. Line a mini-muffin pan with 20 mini paper nonstick liners.
2. In a saucepan, combine coconut butter and coconut oil over low heat. Stir until melted and smooth. Stir in shredded coconut and sweetener until combined.
3. Divide mixture among prepared mini muffin cups and freeze about 30 minutes.
4. For the chocolate coating, combine cocoa butter and unsweetened chocolate together in bowl set over a pan of simmering water (do not let the bottom of the bowl touch the water). Stir until melted.
5. Stir in sifted powdered sweetener, and then stir in cocoa powder, until smooth.
6. Remove from heat and stir in vanilla extract.
7. Melt dark chocolate and spoon over the cold coconut filling.
8. Candies can be stored on your counter top for up to a week.

Servings: 20

Nutrition Facts (per serving)
Carbs: 3,75
Fiber: 0,58g
Protein: 0,52g
Fat: 15,56g
Calories: 142,15

Berry Cacao Bombs

Ingredients
1/3 cup coconut butter
1/2 cup coconut oil
1/2 Tbsp. cocoa powder
10 drops of liquid sweetener of your choice
1/3 cup fresh strawberries, diced
1 Tbsp. coconut, unsweetened shredded
water

Directions
1. In a pan placed over the container holding hot water (bain-marie), add the coconut butter, 1/3 cup coconut oil, cocoa powder and a few drops of liquid sweetener of your choice. Heat and stir until fully melted.
2. In a small saucepan, add the fresh strawberries and a few spoonfuls of water. Cook over medium heat until soft. Mash the strawberries with a fork.
3. Add the mashed strawberries to a blender with 1 Tbsp. of melted coconut oil and a few more drops of liquid sweetener of your choice. Blend until smooth.
4. Fill molds with the melted coconut mixture. Add about 1 tsp. of the strawberry mixture into each mold. Sprinkle with a few shreds of coconut.
5. Refrigerate for a couple of hours. Serve and enjoy!!

Servings: 12

Cooking Times
Total Time: 20 minutes

Nutrition Facts (per serving)
Carbs: 0,52g
Fiber: 0,2g
Net Carbs: 0,24g
Protein: 0,14g
Fat: 14,38g
Calories: 126,85

Zesty Candies

Ingredients
1/4 cup cream cheese
1/4 cup heavy cream
1/4 butter
2 Tbsp. virgin coconut oil
1 lime, squeezed
1 tsp. lime extract
sweetener to taste

Directions
1. In a bowl, mix melted cream cheese, butter and coconut oil; whisk until blended. Add the heavy cream and whisk.
2. Squeeze in lime juice and the lime extract. Add sweetener of your choice per taste.
3. Carefully pour into your tray and leave in your freezer overnight.
4. Pop them out of the tray the next morning, Ready!
5. Enjoy!

Servings: 8

Cooking Times
Total Time: 10 minutes

Nutrition Facts (per serving)
Carbs: 0,67g
Fiber: 0,01g
Net Carbs: 0,28g
Protein: 0,62g
Fat: 11,51
Calories: 105,67

Coco-Melon Squares

Ingredients
1 cup coconut butter
1/2 cup melon cubes
1/2 tsp. sweetener of your choice to taste
1/2 tsp. vanilla extract
1 Tbsp. lemon juice

Directions
1. Line a small pan with parchment paper. Set aside.
2. Place melon cubes, coconut butter and coconut oil in a pot and heat over medium heat until well combined. When ready, set aside to cool for 10 minutes.
3. In a blender, add melon mix and remaining Ingredients. Blend until smooth.
4. Spread out into a prepared pan. Refrigerate until mix has hardened.
5. Remove from fridge and cut into squares. Serve.

Servings: 12

Cooking Times
Total Time: 10 minutes

Nutrition Facts (per serving)
Carbs: 0,81g
Fiber: 006g
Net Carbs: 0,65g
Protein: 0,21g
Fat: 15,38g
Calories: 139,11

Dark Love Cups

Ingredients
4 Tbsp. coconut oil (refined)
4 Tbsp. dark chocolate cocoa powder
3 tsp. sweetener of your choice
1 tsp. vanilla extract
Almond butter
Sea salt (optional)

Directions
1. Melt coconut oil in microwave for 45 seconds. In a bowl, stir in cocoa, sweetener of your choice and vanilla; mix until smooth.
2. Pour chocolate mixture into mini silicone cups and spoon a small bit of Almond butter into each cup. Sprinkle with sea salt (optional).
3. Freeze for 30 minutes. Ready for enjoy!

Servings: 4

Cooking Times
Total Time: 10 minutes

Nutrition Facts (per serving)
Carbs: 5,55g
Fiber: 1,8g
Net Carbs: 2,3g
Protein: 1,11g
Fat: 14,34
Calories: 141,95

Coco-Loco Bombs

Ingredients
6 Tbsp. cocoa butter, softened
6 Tbsp. coconut oil melted
2 Tbsp. finely shredded coconut
1 tsp. granulated sweetener of choice, to taste

Directions
1. In a bowl, mix all the Ingredients in a pouring bowl.
2. Pour into ice cube trays or silicon moulds.
3. Refrigerate for 30 minutes.
4. Serve!

Servings: 10

Cooking Times
Total Time: 5 minutes

Nutrition Facts (per serving)
Carbs: 2,12 g
Fiber: 0,02g
Net Carbs: 0,1g
Protein: 0,05g
Fat: 19,04g
Calories: 174,6

Berry Bliss Pieces

Ingredients
1/2 cup cream cheese, at room temperature
1/2 cup coconut oil
1/2 cup heavy whipping cream
1 tsp. pure raspberry extract
10 drops sweetener of choice

Directions
1. With help of an immersion blender, blend together all of the Ingredients.
2. Spread the mixture into a silicone tray and freeze for 2-3 hours.
3. Once hardened, remove from the silicone tray and serve.
4. Enjoy!

Servings: 10

Cooking Times
Total Time: 10 minutes

Nutrition Facts (per serving)
Carbs: 0,89g
Fiber: 0g
Net Carbs: 0,47g
Protein: 0,93g
Fat: 19,27g
Calories: 175,05

Vanilla Cacao Cakes

Ingredients
4 oz cacao butter
2 cup coconut milk
1/2 cup coconut oil
1 cup coconut butter
1/2 cup vanilla protein powder
1 tsp. pure vanilla extract
1 tsp. liquid sweetener of your choice
pinch salt (optional)
unsweetened coconut flakes

Directions
1. Line the 8 by 8 pan with parchment paper.
2. Melt the cacao butter in a sauce pan over low heat.
3. Stir in the coconut oil, coconut butter and coconut milk; stir well until completely smooth.
4. Turn off heat and whisk in the sweetener of your taste, pure vanilla extract, protein powder and salt.
5. Pour mixture into prepared pan.
6. Sprinkle with coconut flakes.
7. Refrigerate overnight.
8. Enjoy!

Servings: 24

Cooking Times
Total Time: 10 minutes

Nutrition Facts (per serving)
Carbs: 1,14g
Fiber: 0g
Net Carbs: 0,03g
Protein: 0,4g
Fat: 21,1g
Calories: 189,64

Citrus Flare Bombs

Ingredients
1/2 cup cream cheese (heavy cream)
1/2 cup coconut oil
1/2 cup heavy whipping cream
1 tsp. pure orange extract
10 drops sweetener of choice

Directions
1. With help of an immersion blender, blend together all of the Ingredients.
2. Spread the mixture into a silicone tray and freeze for 2-3 hours.
3. Once hardened, remove from the silicone tray and serve.
4. Enjoy!

Servings: 10

Cooking Times
Total Time: 5 minutes

Nutrition Facts (per serving)
Carbs: 0,89g
Fiber: 0g
Net Carbs: 0,47g
Protein: 0,93g
Fat: 19,27
Calories: 175,25

Strawberry Dream Bombs

Ingredients
1/3 cup butter
4 Tbsp. coconut oil
2 Tbsp. sugar-free strawberry syrup
3 Tbsp. walnuts, ground
2 Tbsp. cocoa powder

Directions
1. Combine all Ingredients (except ground walnuts) in sauce pan over extremely low heat until chocolate sauce consistency.
2. Make 8 bowls and roll in ground walnuts.
3. Place balls on a serving pan and freeze for at least 2 hours.

Servings: 8

Cooking Times
Total Time: 10 minutes

Nutrition Facts (per serving)
Carbs: 1,17g
Fiber: 0,64g
Net Carbs: 0,1g
Protein: 0,77g
Fat: 16,49g
Calories: 147,9

All-stars Peanut-Butter Cookies

Ingredients
2 cups peanut butter
1/4 cup Erythritol
2 eggs
1 1/4 cups coconut flour
2 tsp. baking soda
2 tsp. peanut extract
1/2 tsp. kosher salt

Directions
1. Preheat oven to 345° F.
2. In a bowl beat the peanut butter, coconut flour and Erythritol with an electric mixer (MEDIUM speed) until fluffy. Reduce speed to LOW and add in the eggs, baking soda, vanilla, and salt.
3. With your hands make balls from the batter and place on parchment-lined baking pan. Bake 10 to 15 minutes. When ready, cool slightly and then move from the stove to cool completely. Ready. Serve.

Servings: 18
Cooking Times
Total Time: 1 hour and 15 minutes

Nutrition Facts (per serving)
Calories 182
Fat 14,67g
Carbs 8,65g
Fiber 1,96g
Protein 7g

Almond Chocolate Brownies

Ingredients
3 eggs
4 oz dark chocolate, unsweetened
1/2 cup coconut oil
1 cup almond flour
1 cup walnuts
2 Tbsp. cocoa, unsweetened
1 tsp. vanilla essence
2 cups granulated sweetener Stevia or Erythritol
1 tsp. baking soda
pinch of salt

Directions
1. Preheat the oven to 350F.
2. In a container, add almond flour, sweetener, cocoa, salt and baking soda. With an electric mixer, blend the Ingredients on the slowest setting until combined well.
3. Melt the chocolate and the coconut oil together (In a microwave or double boiler). Stir thoroughly.
4. Add eggs and vanilla essence to the flour and mix on a medium speed until a thick batter is formed.
5. Add the butter/chocolate mix to the batter continuing on medium speed until an even texture is formed. Line a slice tin or square baking tin with wax paper. Fold in walnut pieces then turn the batter into your slice tin.
6. Bake for 25 minutes. When ready let cool on wire rack.
7. Cut into 16 Brownies and serve.

Servings: 16
Cooking Times: 35 minutes

Nutrition Facts (per serving)
Calories 207
Fat 20,72g
Carbs 5,38g
Fiber 2,82g
Protein 5,14g

Almond Chocolate Cookies

Ingredients
2 cups almond meal
1 1/2 tsp. almond extract
4 Tbsp. cocoa powder
5 Tbsp. coconut oil, melted
2 Tbsp. almond milk
4 Tbsp. agave nectar
2 tsp. vanilla extract
1/8 tsp. baking soda
1/8 tsp. salt

Directions
1. Preheat oven to 340F degrees.
2. In a deep bowl mix salt, cocoa powder, almond meal and baking soda.
3. In a separate bowl, whisk together melted coconut oil, almond milk, almond and vanilla extract and maple syrup. Merge the almond meal mixture with almond milk mixture and mix well.
4. In a greased baking pan pour the batter evenly. Bake for 10-15 minutes. 5. Once ready let cool on a wire rack and serve.

Servings: 12

Cooking Times
Total Time: 25 minutes

Nutrition Facts (per serving)
Calories 79
Fat 5,94g
Carbs 7,02g
Fiber 0,61g
Protein 0,46g

Carrot Flowers Muffins

Ingredients
2 eggs
2 cups shredded carrots
1/4 cup coconut flour
1/2 cup coconut oil
1 tsp. vanilla extract
1/4 cup Erythritol
2 tsp. ground cinnamon
1 tsp. baking powder

Directions
1. Preheat oven to 350F. Prepare12 muffin tins.
2. In your food processor, add in carrots, eggs, coconut oil, Erythritol, and vanilla. Blend together until combined.
3. In a separate bowl, mix together coconut flour, cinnamon and baking powder.
4. Pour the carrot mixture into the dry Ingredients and mix until completely combined.
5. Pour carrot mixture into the muffin tin and bake for about 30-35 minutes.
6. Remove from the oven, and let cool for at least 30 minutes. Serve.

Servings: 12

Cooking Times
Total Time: 50 minutes

Nutrition Facts (per serving)
Calories 127
Fat 10,04g
Carbs 8,81g
Fiber 0,91g
Protein 1,53g

Coconut Jelly Cake

Ingredients
1 cup coconut flour
1/2 cup butter, softened
2 Tbsp. raspberry jelly
1/2 cup coconut sugar
3 cups desiccated coconut
1 egg
2/3 cup coconut milk
1 cup boiling water
1 cup cold water
1/2 cup double thick cream

Directions
1. Preheat oven to 360F. Grease a patty pan.
2. In a bowl beat butter and coconut sugar until light. Add in egg and beat until well combined. Gently fold in half the coconut flour and half the milk. Repeat with remaining flour and milk.
3. Spoon mixture into patty pan. Bake for 15 to 20 minutes. Once ready, let cool cakes on a wire rack.
4. Stir jelly and boiling water together in a bowl until crystals are dissolved. Stir in cold water. Refrigerate for 1 hour.
5. Place coconut into a large bowl. Cut each cake in half. Stick halves back together using 1 teaspoon of cream. Using a slotted spoon lower cakes, 1 cake at a time, into jelly. Drain excess jelly.
6. Toss cakes in coconut until well coated. When ready, place onto a lined tray and refrigerate at least 1 hour or until set.

Servings: 18
Cooking Times: 30 minutes

Nutrition Facts (per serving)
Calories 146
Fat 14,31g
Carbs 4,21g
Fiber 2,16g
Protein 1,83g

Cottage Pumpkin Pie Ice Cream

Ingredients
1/2 cup toasted pecans, chopped
3 egg yolks
2 Tbsp. butter, salted
2 cups coconut milk
1/2 cup pumpkin puree
1 tsp. pumpkin spice
1/2 cup cottage cheese
1/2 tsp. chia seeds
1/3 cup Erythritol
20 drops liquid Nutria

Directions
1. Place all Ingredients into a container of your immersion blender. Blend all of the Ingredients together into a smooth mixture.
2. Add mixture to your ice cream machine, as per instructions of your manufacturer.
3. Follow the churning instructions as per your ice cream maker manufacturer's instructions. Serve in a chilled bowls or glasses.

Servings: 6

Cooking Times
Total Time: 15 minutes

Nutrition Facts (per serving)
Calories 233
Fat 21,74g
Carbs 6,87g
Fiber 1,95g
Protein 5,49g

Divine Chocolate Biscotti

Ingredients
1 egg
2 cups whole almonds
2 Tbsp. flax seeds
1 cup shredded coconut, unsweetened
1 cup coconut oil
1 cup cacao powder
1/4 cup Xylitol or Stevia sweetener
1 tsp. salt
1 tsp. baking soda

Directions
1. Preheat oven to 350F.
2. In a food process blend the whole almonds with the flax seeds. Add in the rest of Ingredients and mix well.
3. Place the dough on a piece of aluminum foil to shape into 8 biscotti-shaped slices. Bake for 12 minutes.
4. Let cool and serve.

Servings: 8

Cooking Times
Total Time: 25 minutes

Nutrition Facts (per serving)
Calories 276,56
Fat 25,44g 39%
Carbs 9,19g 3%
Fiber 5,2g 21%
Protein 8,24g 16%

Halloween Pumpkin Ice Cream

Ingredients
1 cup almond milk (unsweetened)
1 cup coconut milk
1 cup pumpkin puree
2 1/2 tsp. ground cinnamon
1 tsp. pure vanilla extract
1/2 tsp. ground ginger
1/2 tsp. nutmeg
1/8 tsp. sea salt
Thickener:
1/2 tsp. guar gum or 1 tablespoon gelatin dissolved in 1/4 cup boiling water

Directions
1. Put the coconut milk in a blender and purée until smooth.
2. Pour into the ice cream machine or blender and churn well. Serve in chilled glasses.
3. Freeze for about an hour or refrigerate until cold.
4. Add the almond milk, pumpkin puree, vanilla, cinnamon, ginger, nutmeg and salt, plus thickener. Purée until smooth.
5. Serve.

Servings: 6

Cooking Times
Inactive Time: 1 hour
Total Time: 15 minutes

Nutrition Facts (per serving)
Calories 118
Fat 11,3g
Carbs 4,73g
Fiber 1,4g
Protein 1,35g

Hemp and Chia Seeds Cream

Ingredients
1 ¼ cup coconut milk
2 Tbsp. hemp powder
2 sheets of unflavored gelatin
3 Tbsp. chia seeds

Directions
1. In a saucepan over low heat add the coconut milk and dissolve the lucuma powder.
2. Cut the gelatin into pieces and add it to the milk. Stir until dissolved completely.
3. Add chia seeds and stir occasionally until mixture thickens, about 15 minutes. Pour the mixture into individual containers and allow cool before putting them in the refrigerator for at least 2 hours before serving. Enjoy!

Servings: 3

Cooking Times
Total Time: 20 minutes

Nutrition Facts (per serving)
Calories 202
Fat 19,2g
Carbs 8,12g
Fiber 3,14g
Protein 2,59g

Homemade Nuts Bars

Ingredients
1 cup almonds
1/2 cup hazelnut, chopped
1 cup peanuts
1 cup shredded coconut
1 cup almond butter
1 cup Liquid Erythritol
1 cup coconut oil, freshly melted and still warm

Directions
1. In a food processor place all nuts and chop for 1-2 minutes.
2. Add in grated coconut, almond butter, Erythritol and coconut oil. Process it for 1 minute about.
3. Cover a square bowl with parchment paper and place the mixture on top.
4. Flatten the mixture with a spatula. Place the bowl in the freezer for 4-5 hours.
5. Remove batter from the freezer, cut and serve.

Servings: 10

Cooking Times
Cooking Time: 10 minutes
Inactive Time: 5 hours

Nutrition Facts (per serving)
Calories 193
Fat 18,2g
Carbs 6,64g
Fiber 2,53g
Protein 3,83g

Creamy Avocado Smoothie

Ingredients
1 Haas avocado
3 oz almond milk, unsweetened
3 oz heavy whipping cream
6 drops Liquid Stevia
Ice cubes

Directions
1. Cut the avocado in half, remove the seed and remove the flesh from the skin.
2. In a blender mix the almond milk, avocado, heavy whipping cream, sweetener and ice cubes. Blend 1 minute.
3. Serve.

Servings: 3

Cooking Times
Total Time: 7 minutes

Nutrition Facts (per serving)
Calories 252
Fat 24,43g
Carbs 8,31g
Fiber 5,51g
Protein 3,69g

Caramel Coffee Smoothie

Ingredients

1/2 cup heavy cream
1/2 cup almond milk, unsweetened
3 Tbsp. sugar-free chocolate syrup
3 Tbsp. sugar-free caramel syrup
3/4 cup cold coffee
2 Tbsp. cocoa, unsweetened
Ice cubes

Directions

1. In a blender add all Ingredients and blend until all incorporate well.
2. Pour in glasses and serve.

Servings: 4

Cooking Times
Total Time: 5 minutes

Nutrition Facts (per serving)
Calories 170
Fat 14,95g
Carbs 9,02g
Fiber 1,92g
Protein 2,8g

Chia Seed Cream

Ingredients
1/4 cup Chia seeds
1 cup heavy whipping cream
1 cup coconut milk
2 Tbsp. cocoa powder
pure vanilla extract
1/4 cup Erythritol sweetener

Directions
1. In a bowl mix the chia seeds and add the coconut milk until it combines well.
2. Add the Erythritol and whisk some more. Divide the mixture into two portions.
3. Add cocoa to one half and mixed it nicely.
4. Pour chia seed mixture into the bowls or glasses. Keep covered in the refrigerator for 12 hours.
5. Before serving beat the heavy whipping cream and pour over the chia seeds cream. Enjoy!

Servings: 4

Cooking Times
Total Time: 12 hours

Nutrition Facts (per serving)
Calories 341
Fat 35,41g
Carbs 7,35g
Fiber 1,56g
Protein 2,99g

Chocolate Brownies

Ingredients
2 eggs
1 1/2 cups almond flour
1/4 cup coconut oil
1/2 cup cocoa powder, unsweetened
1 Tbsp. Metamucil Fiber Powder
1/3 cup Natvia (or some other natural sweetener)l
1/4 cup maple syrup
1 tsp. baking powder
1/2 tsp. salt

Directions
1. Preheat oven to 350F.
2. In a bowl add in all wet Ingredients and 2 Eggs. Beat the wet Ingredients together using a hand mixer until a consistent mixture is formed.
3. In a separate bowl, combine all dry Ingredients. Mix the dry Ingredients well. Pour the wet Ingredients slowly into the dry Ingredients, mixing with a hand mixer as you pour.
4. Pour the batter into baking pan. Bake the brownies for 20 minutes.
5. When ready, let the brownies cool. Slice brownies into slices and serve.

Servings: 10

Cooking Times
Total Time: 35 minutes

Nutrition Facts (per serving)
Calories 157
Fat 13,4g
Carbs 8,07g
Fiber 2,58g
Protein 5,04g

Chocolate Pecan Bites

Ingredients
2 oz 100% dark chocolate
2.5 oz pecan halves
cinnamon
nutmeg

Directions
1. Preheat oven to 350F.
2. Place the pecan halves on a parchment paper and bake in oven for 6-7 minutes. When ready, let cool and set aside.
3. Melt the dark chocolate.
4. Dip each pecan half in the melted dark chocolate and place back on the parchment paper.
5. Sprinkle a cinnamon and nutmeg on top of the chocolate covered pecans.
6. Before serving place in refrigerator for 2-3 hours.

Servings: 12

Cooking Times
Total Time: 3 hours

Nutrition Facts (per serving)
Calories 52
Fat 4,96g
Carbs 2,32g
Fiber 0,71g
Protein 0,64g

Hazelnuts Chocolate Cream

Ingredients
1 cup hazelnuts halves
4 Tbsp. unsweetened cocoa powder
1 tsp. pure vanilla extract
2 Tbsp. coconut oil
4 Tbsp. granulated Stevia (or sweetener of choice)

Directions
1. Place all the Ingredients in your blender. Blend until smooth well.
2. Store in the fridge for 1 hour. Serve and enjoy!

Servings: 4
Cooking Times
Total Time: 5 minutes

Nutrition Facts (per serving)
Calories 302
Fat 29g
Carbs 9,5g
Fiber 5,12g
Protein 6,39g

Instant Coffee Ice Cream

Ingredients
1 Tbsp. Instant Coffee
2 Tbsp. Cocoa Powder
1 cup coconut milk
1/4 cup heavy cream
1/4 tsp. flax seeds
2 Tbsp. Erythritol
15 drops liquid Nutria

Directions
1. Add all Ingredients except the flax seeds into a container of your immersion blender.
2. Blend well until all Ingredients are incorporated well. Slowly add in flax seeds until a slightly thicker mixture is formed. Add the mass to your ice cream machine and follow manufacturer's instructions.
3. Ready! Serve!

Servings: 2

Cooking Times
Total Time: 20 minutes

Nutrition Facts (per serving)
Calories 286
Fat 29,21g
Carbs 9,39g
Fiber 1,88g
Protein 3,18g

Jam "Eye" Cookies

Ingredients
2 eggs
1 cup almond flour
2 Tbsp. coconut flour
2 Tbsp. sugar-free jam per taste
1/2 cup natural sweetener (Stevia, Truvia, Erythritol...etc.)
4 Tbsp. coconut oil
1/2 tsp. pure vanilla extract
1/2 tsp. almond extract
1 Tbsp. shredded coconut
1/2 tsp. baking powder
1/4 tsp. cinnamon
1/2 tsp. salt

Directions
1. Preheat your oven to 350F. In a big bowl, combine all your dry Ingredients and whisk.
2. Add in your wet Ingredients and combine well using hand mixer or a whisk.
3. With your hand for make the patties and place the cookies on a parchment paper lined baking sheet. Using your finger make an indent in the middle if each cookie.
4. Bake for about 16 minutes or until the cookies turn golden.
5. Once ready, let the cookies cool on a wire rack and fill each indent with sugar free jam.
6. Before serving sprinkle some shredded coconut on top of each cookie. Enjoy!

Servings: 16
Cooking Time: 36 minutes

Nutrition Facts (per serving)
Calories 95
Fat 8,61g
Carbs 2,79g
Fiber 1,02g
Protein 2,71g

Lemon Coconut Pearls

Ingredients

3 packages of True Lemon (Crystallized Citrus for Water)
1/4 cup shredded coconut, unsweetened
1 cup cream cheese
1/4 cup granulated Stevia

Directions

1. In a bowl, combine cream cheese, lemon and Stevia. Blend well until incorporate.
2. Once the mixture is well combined, put it back in the fridge to harden up a bit.
3. Roll into 16 balls and dip each ball into shredded coconut. Refrigerate for several hours. Serve.

Servings: 4

Cooking Times
Total Time: 15 minutes

Nutrition Facts (per serving)
Calories 216
Fat 21,53g
Carbs 3,12g
Fiber 0,45g
Protein 3,61g

Lime & Vanilla Cheesecake

Ingredients
1/4 cup cream cheese, softened
2 Tbsp. heavy cream
1 tsp. lime juice
1 egg
1 tsp. pure vanilla extract
2-4 Tbsp. Erythritol or Stevia

Directions
1. In a microwave-safe bowl combine all Ingredients. Place in a microwave and cook on HIGH for 90 seconds.
2. Every 30 seconds stir to combine the Ingredients well.
3. Transfer mixture to a bowl and refrigerate for at least 2 hours.
4. Before serving top with whipped cream or coconut powder.

Servings: 2

Cooking Times
Preparation Time: 5 minutes
Inactive Time: 2 hours

Nutrition Facts (per serving)
Calories 140
Fat 13,04g
Carbs 1,38g
Fiber 0,01g
Protein 4,34g

Chocolate Mousse

Ingredients
1/4 cup of heavy cream
1 1/4 cup coconut cream
2 Tbsp. of cocoa powder
3 Tbsp. of Erythritol (or Stevia)
1 Tbsp. pure vanilla essence
shredded coconut, unsweetened

Directions
1. Scoop out the hardened coconut cream from the can, leaving the clear liquid behind, and place into a bowl. Add the heavy cream and combine with a hand mixer on low speed.
2. Add the remaining Ingredients and mix on low speed for 2-3 minutes until the mix is thick.
3. Serve in individual ramekins sprinkled with unsweetened shredded coconut.

Servings: 4
Cooking Times: 15 minutes

Nutrition Facts (per serving)
Calories 305
Fat 31,91g
Carbs 6,97g
Fiber 2,55g
Protein 3,56g

Strawberry Pudding

Ingredients
4 egg yolks
2 Tbsp. butter
1/4 cup coconut flour
2 Tbsp. heavy cream
1/4 cup strawberries
1/4 tsp. baking powder
2 Tbsp. coconut oil
2 tsp. lemon juice
Zest 1 Lemon
2 Tbsp. Erythritol
10 drops Liquid Stevia

Directions
1. Preheat oven to 350F.
2. In a bowl beat the egg yolks with electric mixer until they're pale in color. Add in Erythritol and 10 drops liquid Stevia. Beat again until fully combined.
3. Add in heavy cream, lemon juice, and the zest of 1 lemon. Add the coconut and butter. Beat well until no lumps are found.
4. Sift the dry Ingredients over the wet Ingredients, then mix well on a slow speed.
5. Distribute the strawberries evenly in the batter by pushing them into the top of the batter.
6. Bake for 20-25 minutes. Once finished, let cool for 5 minutes and serve.

Servings: 3
Cooking Times
Total Time: 35 minutes

Nutrition Facts (per serving)
Calories 258
Fat 23,46g
Carbs 9,3g
Fiber 0,61g
Protein 3,98g

Kiwi Fiend Ice Cream

Ingredients
3 egg yolks
1 1/2 cup Kiwi, pureed
1 cup heavy cream
1/3 cup Erythritol
1/2 tsp. pure vanilla extract
1/8 tsp. chia seeds

Directions
1. In a sauce pan heat up the heavy cream. Add in 1/3 cup of erythritol to dissolve; simmer gently until erythritol is dissolved.
2. In a mixing bowl beat 3 egg yolks with an electric mixer. Add in a few tablespoons of your hot cream mixture at a time to the eggs while beating. Add in some pure vanilla extract and mix. Add in 1/8 tsp. of chia seeds.
3. Place your bowl into the freezer to chill for about 1-2 hours, stirring occasionally.
4. In a meanwhile puree the kiwi no more than 1-2 seconds. When the ice cream is chilled and getting a bit thicker, add in kiwi mixture to the chilled cream. Mix a bit.
5. Let the kiwi ice cream to chill at least 6-8 hours. Serve in chilled glasses.

Servings: 6

Cooking Times
Cooking Time: 15 minutes
Total Time: 8 hours and 15 minutes

Nutrition Facts (per serving)
Calories 192
Fat 17,2g
Carbs 8,13g
Fiber 1,46g
Protein 2,69g

Minty Avocado Lime Sorbet

Ingredients
1 cup coconut milk
2 avocados
1/4 mint leaves, chopped
1/4 cup powdered Erythritol
2 limes, juiced
1/4 tsp. liquid Stevia

Directions
1. Slice avocado half vertically through the flesh, making about 5 slices per half of an avocado. Use a spoon to carefully scoop out the pieces. Rest pieces on foil and squeeze juice of 1/2 lime over the tops.
2. Store avocado in freezer for at least 3 hours.
3. Using a spice grinder, powder Erythritol.
4. In a pan, bring coconut milk to a boil.
5. Zest the 2 limes you have while coconut milk is heating up. Add lime zest and continue to let the milk reduce in volume.
6. Remove and place the coconut milk into a container and store in the freezer.
7. Chop mint leaves. Remove avocados from freezer.
8. Add avocado, mint leaves, and juice from lime into the food processor. Pulse until a chunky consistency is achieved.
9. Pour coconut milk mixture over the avocados in the food processor. Add Liquid Stevia to this.
10. Pulse mixture together about 2-3 minutes.
11. Return to freezer to freeze, or serve immediately!

Servings: 6
Cooking Times: 3 hours and 15 minutes

Nutrition Facts (per serving)
Calories 184
Fat 17,26g
Carbs 9,65g
Fiber 4,59g
Protein 1,95g

Morning Zephyr Cake

Ingredients
3 Tbsp. coconut oil
2 Tbsp. grounded flax seeds
8 Tbsp. almonds, grounded
1 cup Greek Yogurt
1 Tbsp. cocoa powder for dusting
1 cup heavy whipping cream
1 tsp. Baking Powder
1 tsp. Baking Soda
1 tsp. pure vanilla essence
1 pinch pink salt
1 cup Stevia or Erythritol sweetener

Directions
1. Pre-heat the oven at 350 F degrees.
2. In the blender first add the grounded almonds, grounded flax seeds and the baking powder and soda. Blend for a minute.
3. Add the salt, coconut oil and blend some more. Add the sweetener and blend for 2-3 minutes.
4. Add the Greek yogurt and blend for a minute or so, until a fine consistency is reached.
5. Take out the batter in a bowl and add the vanilla essence, and mix with a light hand.
6. Grease the baking dish and drop the batter in it.
7. Bake for 30 minutes. Let cool on a wire rack. Serve.

Servings: 8

Cooking Times
Total Time: 40 minutes

Nutrition Facts (per serving)
Calories 199
Fat 20,69g
Carbs 3,22g
Fiber 1,17g
Protein 2,56g

Almond Butter Balls

Ingredients
2 eggs
2 1/2 cup of peanut butter
1/2 cup shredded coconut (unsweetened)
1/2 cup of Xylitol
1 Tbsp. of pure vanilla extract

Directions
1. Preheat oven to 320 F.
2. Mix all Ingredients together by your hands.
3. After the Ingredients are thoroughly mixed, roll into heaped tablespoon sized balls and press into a baking tray lined with baking paper.
4. Bake in the oven for 12 minutes or until the tops of the cookies are browning. When ready, let cool on a wire rack. Ready! Serve.

Servings: 16

Cooking Times
Total Time: 22 minutes

Nutrition Facts (per serving)
Calories 254
Fat 21,75g
Carbs 8,31g
Fiber 2,64g
Protein 10,98g

Pecan Flax Seed Blondie's

Ingredients
3 eggs
2 1/4 cups pecans, roasted
3 Tbsp. heavy cream
1 Tbsp. salted caramel syrup
1/2 cup flax seeds, ground
1/4 cup butter, melted
1/4 cup erythritol, powdered
10 drops Liquid Stevia
1 tsp. baking powder
1 pinch salt

Directions
1. Preheat oven to 350F.
2. In a baking pan roast pecans for 10 minutes.
3. Grind 1/2 cup flax seeds in a spice grinder. Place flax seed powder in a bowl. Grind Erythritol in a spice grinder until powdered. Set in the same bowl as the flax seeds meal.
4. Place 2/3 of roasted pecans in food processor and process until a smooth nut butter is formed.
5. Add eggs, liquid Stevia, salted caramel syrup, and a pinch of salt to the flax seed mixture. Mix well. Add pecan butter to the batter and mix again.
6. Smash the rest of the roasted pecans into chunks. Add crushed pecans and 1/4 cup melted butter into the batter. Mix batter well, and then add heavy cream and baking powder. Mix everything together well.
7. Place the batter into baking tray and bake for 20 minute. Let cool for about 10 minutes. Slice off the edges of the brownie to create a uniform square. Serve.

Servings: 16
Cooking Times: 40 minutes

Nutrition Facts (per serving)
Calories 180
Fat 18,23g
Carbs 3,54g
Fiber 1,78g
Protein 3,07g

Peppermint Chocolate Ice Cream

Ingredients
1/2 tsp. Peppermint extract
1 cup heavy cream
1 cup cheese cream
1 tsp. pure vanilla extract
1 tsp. Liquid Stevia extract
100% Dark Chocolate for topping

Directions
1. Place ice cream bowl in freezer per ice cream maker instructions. In a metal bowl, put all Ingredients except chocolate and whisk well.
2. Put back in freezer for 5 minutes. Setup ice cream maker and add liquid.
3. Before serving, top the ice cream with chocolate shavings. Serve.

Servings: 3

Cooking Times
Total Time: 35 minutes

Nutrition Facts (per serving)
Calories 286
Fat 29,96g
Carbs 2,7g
Fiber 0g
Protein 2,6g

Puff-up Coconut Waffles

Ingredients

1 cup coconut flour
1/2 cup heavy (whipping) cream
5 eggs
1/4 tsp. pink salt
1/4 tsp. baking soda
1/4 cup coconut milk
2 tsp. Yacon Syrup (or some other natural sweetener)
2 Tbsp. coconut oil (melted)

Directions

1. In a large bowl add the eggs and beat with an electric hand mixer for 30 seconds.
2. Add the heavy (whipping) cream and coconut oil into the eggs while you are still mixing. Add the coconut milk, coconut flour, pink salt and baking soda. Mix with the hand mixer for 45 second on low speed. Set aside.
3. Heat up your waffle maker well and make the waffles according to your manufactures specifications.
4. Serve hot.

Servings: 8

Nutrition Facts (per serving)
Calories 169
Fat 12,6g
Carbs 9,97g
Fiber 0,45g
Sugar 0,38g
Protein 4,39g

Raspberry Chocolate Cream

Ingredients
1/2 cup 100% dark chocolate, chopped
1/4 cup of heavy cream
1/2 cup cream cheese, softened
2 Tbsp. sugar free Raspberry Syrup
1/4 cup Erythritol

Directions
1. In a double boiler melt chopped chocolate and the cream cheese. Add the Erythritol sweetener and continue to stir. Remove from heat, let cool and set aside.
2. When the cream has cooled add in heavy cream and Raspberry syrup and stir well.
3. Pour cream in a bowls or glasses and serve. Keep refrigerated.

Servings: 4

Cooking Times
Total Time: 15 minutes

Nutrition Facts (per serving)
Calories 157
Fat 13,51g
Carbs 7,47g
Fiber 1g
Protein 1,95g

Raw Cacao Hazelnut Cookies

Ingredients
2 cups almond flour
1 cup chopped hazelnut
1/2 cup cacao powder
1/2 cup ground flax
3 Tbsp. coconut oil (melted)
1/3 cup water
1/3 cup Erythritol
1/4 tsp. liquid Stevia

Directions
1. In a bowl, mix almond flour and flax and cacao powder. Stir in oil, water, agave and vanilla. When it is well mixed, stir in chopped hazelnuts.
2. Form in to balls, press flat with palms and place on dehydrator screens.
3. Dehydrate 1 hour at 145, then reduce to 116 and dehydrate for at least 5 hours or until desired dryness is achieved.
4. Serve.

Servings: 24

Cooking Times
Total Time: 6 hours

Nutrition Facts (per serving)
Calories 181
Fat 15,69g
Carbs 8,75g
Fiber 3,45g
Protein 4,46g

Sinless Pumpkin Cheesecake Muffins

Ingredients
1/2 cup pureed pumpkin
1 tsp. pumpkin pie spice
1/2 cup pecans, finely ground
1/2 cup cream cheese
1 Tbsp. coconut oil
1/2 tsp. pure vanilla extract
1/4 tsp. pure Yacon Syrup or Erythritol

Directions
1. Prepare a muffin tin with liners.
2. Place a small amount of ground pecans into every muffin tin and make a thin crust.
3. In a bowl, blend sweetener, spices, vanilla, coconut and the pumpkin puree. Add in the cream cheese and beat until the mixture is well combined.
4. Scoop about two tablespoons of filling mixture on top of each crust, and smooth around the edges.
5. Pop in the freezer for about 45 minutes.
6. Remove from the muffin tin and let sit for 10 minutes. Serve.

Servings: 6

Cooking Times
Total Time: 15 minutes

Nutrition Facts (per serving)
Calories 157
Fat 15,52g
Carbs 3,94g
Fiber 1,51g
Protein 2,22g

Sour Hazelnuts Biscuits with Arrowroot Tea

Ingredients
1 egg
1/2 cup hazelnuts
3 Tbsp. of coconut oil
2 cups almond flour
2 Tbsp. of arrowroot tea
2 tsp. ginger
1 Tbsp. cocoa powder
1/2 cup grapefruit juice
1 orange peel from a half orange
1/2 tsp. baking soda
1 pinch of salt

Directions
1. Preheat oven to 360 °F. Make arrowroot tea and let it cool.
2. In a food processor blend the hazelnuts. Add the remaining Ingredients and continue blending until mixed well. With your hands form a cookies with the batter.
3. Put the cookies on baking parchment paper, and bake for 30-35 minutes. When ready, remove tray from the oven and let cool.
4. Serve warm or cold.

Servings: 12

Cooking Times
Total Time: 50 minutes

Nutrition Facts (per serving)
Calories 224
Fat 20,17g
Carbs 8,06g
Fiber 3,25g
Protein 6,36g

Tartar Cookies

Ingredients
3 eggs
1/8 tsp. cream of tartar
1/3 cup cream cheese
1/8 tsp. salt
some oil for greasing

Directions
1. Preheat oven to 300°F. Line the cookie sheet with parchment paper and grease with some oil.
2. Separate eggs from the egg yolks. Set both in different mixing bowls.
3. With an electric hand mixer, start beating the egg whites until super bubbly. Add in cream of tartar and beat until stiff peaks form.
4. In the egg yolk bowl, add in cream cheese and some salt. Beat until the egg yolks are pale yellow.
5. Merge the egg whites into the cream cheese mixture. Stir well.
6. Make cookies and place on the cookie sheet.
7. Bake for about 30-40 minutes. When ready, let them cool on a wire rack and serve.

Servings: 8

Cooking Times
Total Time: 35 minutes

Nutrition Facts (per serving)
Calories 59,99
Fat 5,09g
Carbs 0,56g
Fiber 0g
Protein 2,93g

Wild Strawberries Ice Cream

Ingredients
1/2 cup wild strawberries
1/3 cup cream cheese
1 cup heavy cream
1 Tbsp. lemon juice
1 tsp. pure vanilla extract
1/3 cup of your favorite sweetener
Ice cubes

Directions
1. Place all Ingredients in a blender. Blend until all incorporate well.
2. Refrigerate for 2-3 hour before serving.

Servings: 4

Cooking Times
Total Time: 5 minutes

Nutrition Facts
Calories 176,43
Fat 17,69g
Carbs 3,37g
Fiber 0,39g
Protein 1,9g

Mini Lemon Cheesecakes

Ingredients
1 tablespoon lemon zest, grated
1 teaspoon lemon juice
½ teaspoon stevia powder or (Truvia)
1/4 cup coconut oil, softened
4 tablespoons unsalted butter, softened
4 ounces cream cheese (heavy cream)

Directions
1. Blend all Ingredients together with a hand mixer or blender until smooth and creamy.
2. Prepare a cupcake or muffin tin with 6 paper liners.
3. Pour mixture into prepared tin and place in freezer for 2-3 hours or until firm.
4. Sprinkle cups with additional lemon zest. Or try using chopped nuts or shredded, unsweetened coconut.

Serves: 6

Cooking Times
Total Time: 5 minutes

Calories: 196
Fat: 21.2 grams

Chocolate Layered Coconut Cups

Ingredients

Bottom Layer:
1/2 cup unsweetened, shredded coconut
3 tablespoons powdered sweetener such as Splenda or Truvia
1/2 cup coconut butter
1/2 cup coconut oil

Top Layer:
1 1/2 ounces cocoa butter
1 ounce unsweetened chocolate
1/4 cup cocoa powder
1/2 teaspoon vanilla extract
1/4 cup powdered sweetener such as Splenda or Truvia

Directions
1. Prepare a mini-muffin pan with 20 mini paper liners.
2. For the bottom layer:
3. Combine coconut butter and coconut oil in a small saucepan over low heat. Stir until smooth and melted then add the shredded coconut and powdered sweetener until combined.
4. Divide the mixture among prepared mini muffin cups and freeze until firm, about 30 minutes.
5. For the top layer:
6. Combine cocoa butter and unsweetened chocolate together in double boiler or a bowl set over a pan of simmering water. Stir until melted.
7. Stir in the powdered sweetener, then the cocoa powder and mix until smooth.
8. Remove from heat and stir in the vanilla extract.
9. Spoon chocolate topping over chilled coconut candies and let set, about 15 minutes. Enjoy!

Serves: 10
Serving Size: 2 pieces

Calories: 240
Fat: 25 grams

Pumpkin Pie Chocolate Cups

Ingredients
Для the crust:
3.5 ounces extra dark chocolate - 85% cocoa solids or more
2 tablespoons coconut oil

For the pie:
½ cup coconut butter
¼ cup coconut oil
2 teaspoons pumpkin pie spice mix
½ cup unsweetened pumpkin puree
2 tablespoons healthy low-carb sweetener
Optional: 15-20 drops liquid stevia for added sweetness

Directions
1. Place the chocolate and coconut oil in a double boiler or a glass bowl on top of a small saucepan filled with simmering water. Once completely melted, remove from the heat and set aside.
2. Prepare a mini muffin tin with 18 paper liners. Fill each of the 18 mini muffin cups with 2 teaspoons of the chocolate mixture. Place the chocolate in the fridge to set up for at least 10 minutes.
3. Place the coconut butter, coconut oil, sweetener and pumpkin spice mix into a bowl and melt just like you did the chocolate.
4. Add the pumpkin puree and mix until smooth and well combined.
5. Remove the muffin cups from the fridge and add a heaping teaspoon of the pumpkin & coconut mixture into every cup. Place back in the fridge and let it set for at least 30 minutes.
6. When done, keep refrigerated. Coconut oil and butter get very soft at room temperature. Store in the fridge for up to a week or freeze for up to 3 months. Enjoy!

Serves: 18
Serving Size: 1 mini pie

Calories: 110
Fat: 10.9 grams

Fudgy Slow Cooker Cake

Ingredients
1 1/2 cups almond flour
1/4 cup whey protein powder(chocolate, vanilla, unflavored all work fine)
3/4 cup sugar substitute such as Swerve or Truvia
2/3 cup cocoa powder
2 teaspoons baking powder
1/4 teaspoon sea salt
1/2 cup butter, melted
4 large eggs
3/4 cup almond or coconut milk, unsweetened
1 teaspoon vanilla extract
1/2 cup chopped dark chocolate, 85% cocoa or higher
<u>Whipped cream topping (optional):</u>
1/2 cup heavy whipping cream
2 tablespoons sugar substitute

Directions
1. Grease the insert of a 6 quart slow cooker well with butter or coconut oil.
2. In a medium bowl, whisk together almond flour, sugar substitute, cocoa powder, whey protein powder, baking powder and salt.
3. Stir in butter, eggs, almond milk and vanilla extract until well combined, then fold in the chopped dark chocolate.
4. Pour into the greased slow cooker and cook on low for 2.5 to 3 hours. It will be gooey and like a pudding cake at 2.5 hours, and little more cake like at 3 hours.
5. Turn slow cooker off and let cool for 20 to 30 minutes. Cut into pieces and serve warm.
6. Best when served with freshly whipped cream. To make this, mix the whipping cream and sugar substitute together with your stand mixer, or a hand mixer. Continue mixing until soft peaks form.

Serves: 10
Serving Size: 1/10th of cake

Calories: 275
Fat: 23

Easy Sticky Chocolate Fudge

Ingredients
1 cup coconut oil, softened
1/4 cup coconut milk (full fat, from a can)
1/4 cup cocoa powder
1 teaspoon vanilla extract
1/2 teaspoon sea salt
1-3 drops liquid stevia

Directions
1. With a hand mixer or stand mixer, whip the softened coconut oil and coconut milk together until smooth and glossy. About 6 minutes on high.
2. Add the cocoa powder, vanilla extract, sea salt, and one drop of liquid stevia to the bowl and mix on low until combined. Increase speed once everything is combined and mix for one minute. Taste fudge and adjust sweetness by adding additional liquid stevia, if desired.
3. Prepare a 9"x4" loaf pan by lining it with parchment paper.
4. Pour fudge into loaf pan and place in freezer for about 15, until just set.
5. Remove fudge and cut into 1" x 1" pieces. Store in an airtight container in the fridge or freezer.

Serves: 12
Serving Size: (2) 1" pieces

Calories: 172
Fat: 19.6 grams

Strawberry Cheesecake Ice Cream Cups

Ingredients

1/2 strawberries, fresh or frozen, mashed well
3/4 cup cream cheese, softened
1/4 cup coconut oil, softened
10-15 drops liquid stevia
1 teaspoon vanilla extract

Directions
1. Combine all Ingredients in a medium sized bowl and mix with a hand mixer until smooth and creamy. Can also be done in a food processor or high speed blender.)
2. Spoon the mixture into mini muffin silicon molds or small candy molds. Place in the freezer for about 2 hours or until set.
3. When done, unmold the Fatbombs and place into a container. Keep in the freezer and enjoy any time!

Serves: 12
Serving Size: 1 bite

Calories: 67
Fat: 7.4 grams

English Toffee Treats

Ingredients

1 cup coconut oil
2 tablespoons butter
1/2 block cream cheese, softened
3/4 tablespoons cocoa powder
1/2 cup creamy, natural peanut butter
3 tablespoons Davinci Gourmet Sugar Free English Toffee Syrup

Directions

1. Combine all Ingredients in a saucepan over medium heat.
2. Stir until everything is smooth, melted, and combined.
3. Pour mixture into small candy molds or mini muffin tins lined with paper liners.
4. Freeze or refrigerate until set and enjoy!
5. Store in an airtight container in the fridge.

Serves: 24
Serving Size: 1 piece
Calories: 142
Fat: 15 grams

Fudgy Almond Butter Squares

Ingredients

1 cup all natural creamy peanut butter
1 cup coconut oil
1/4 cup unsweetened vanilla almond milk
a pinch of coarse sea salt
1 teaspoon vanilla extract
2 teaspoons liquid stevia (optional)

Directions

1. In a microwave safe bowl, soften the Almond butter and coconut oil together. (About 1 minute on med-low heat.)
2. Combine the softened Almond butter and coconut oil with the remaining Ingredients into a blender or food processor.
3. Blend until thoroughly combined.
4. Pour into a 9X4" loaf pan that has been lined with parchment paper.
5. Refrigerate until set. About 2 hours.
6. Enjoy!

Serves: 12
Serving Size: (2) 1" pieces

Calories: 287
Fat: 29.7

Peppermint Patties

Ingredients
¾ cup melted coconut butter
¼ cup finely shredded, unsweetened coconut
2 tablespoons cacao powder
3 tablespoons coconut oil, melted
½ teaspoon pure peppermint extract

Directions
1. Mix together melted coconut butter, shredded coconut, 1 tablespoon of coconut oil and peppermint extract
2. Pour coconut butter mixture into mini muffin tins that have been lined with paper liners. Fill half way.
3. Place in refrigerator and allow to harden for about 15 minutes.
4. Mix together 2 tablespoons coconut oil and cacao powder.
5. Remove muffin tin from refrigerator and top each one with chocolate mixture.
6. Return to refrigerator until the chocolate has set.
7. When ready to eat, simply set the peppermint patty cups on the counter for about 5 minutes and unmold from muffin tin.

Serves: 12
Serving Size: 2 pieces

Calories: 80
Fat: 7 grams

Buttery Pecan Delights

Ingredients

8 pecan halves
1 tablespoon unsalted butter, softened
2 ounces neufchâtel cheese
1 teaspoon orange zest, finely grated
pinch of sea salt

Directions
1. Toast the pecans at 350 degrees Fahrenheit for 5-10 minutes, check often to prevent burning.
2. Mix the butter, neufchâtel cheese, and orange zest until smooth and creamy.
3. Spread the butter mixture between the cooled pecan halves and sandwich together.
4. Sprinkle with sea salt and enjoy!

Serves: 2
Serving Size: 2 pecan sandwiches

Calories: 163
Fat: 16 grams

Fudge Oh So Chocolate

Ingredients
1 cup coconut oil, softened
1/4 cup coconut milk (full fat, from a can)
1/2 teaspoon sea salt
1-3 drops liquid stevia
1/4 cup cocoa powder
1 teaspoon vanilla extract

Directions
1. With a hand mixer or stand mixer, whip the softened coconut oil and coconut milk together until smooth and glossy. About 6 minutes on high.
2. Add the cocoa powder, vanilla extract, sea salt, and one drop of liquid stevia to the bowl and mix on low until combined. Increase speed once everything is combined and mix for one minute. Taste fudge and adjust sweetness by adding additional liquid stevia, if desired.
3. Prepare a 9"x4" loaf pan by lining it with parchment paper.
4. Pour fudge into loaf pan and place in freezer for about 15, until just set.
5. Remove fudge and cut into 1" x 1" pieces. Store in an airtight container in the fridge or freezer.

Serves: 12
Serving Size: (2) 1" pieces

Calories: 172
Fat: 19.6 grams

Cinna-Bun Balls

Ingredients
1 cup coconut butter
1 teaspoon vanilla extract
1 cup full Fat coconut milk (from a can)
1 cup unsweetened coconut shreds
1/2 teaspoon cinnamon
1/2 teaspoon nutmeg
1 teaspoon sugar substitute such as Splenda

Directions
1. Combine all Ingredients except the shredded coconut together in double boiler or a bowl set over a pan of simmering water. Stir until everything is melted and combined.
2. Remove bowl from heat and place in the fridge until the mixture has firmed up and can be rolled into balls.
3. Form the mixture into 1" balls, a small cookie scoop is helpful for doing this.
4. Roll each ball in the shredded coconut until well coated.
5. Serve and enjoy! Store in the fridge.

Serves: 10
Serving Size: 1 ball
Calories: 273
Fat: 30.9 grams

Vanilla Mousse Cups

Ingredients
8 ounces (1 block) cream cheese, softened
1/2 cup sugar substitute such as Swerve or Truvia (Stevia)
1 1/2 teaspoons vanilla extract
dash of sea salt
1/2 cup heavy whipping cream

Directions
1. Add the first four Ingredients to a food processor or blender.
2. Blend until combined.
3. With blender running, slowly add the heavy cream.
4. Continue to blend until thickened, about 1-2 minutes. Consistency should be mousse like.
5. Prepare a cupcake or muffin tin with 6 paper liners and portion the mixture into the cups.
6. Chill in the fridge until set and enjoy!

Serves: 6
Serving Size: 1 piece

Calories: 199
Fat: 20.2 grams

Conclusion

Thank you again for downloading this book!

I hope this book was able to inspire you to get into the kitchen and whip up some delectable, LCHF desserts!

When you make these recipes, please share them with your friends and family, let them know about the book, and encourage them not to be intimidated by LCHF foods.

Finally, if you enjoyed this book, please take the time to share your thoughts and post a review on Amazon. It's greatly appreciated!

Thank you and bon appétit!

© Copyright 2016 by –Will Kenton- All rights reserved.

This document is geared towards providing exact and reliable information in regards to the topic and issue covered. The publication is sold with the idea that the publisher is not required to render accounting, officially permitted, or otherwise, qualified services. If advice is necessary, legal or professional, a practiced individual in the profession should be ordered.

- From a Declaration of Principles which was accepted and approved equally by a Committee of the American Bar Association and a Committee of Publishers and Associations.

In no way is it legal to reproduce, duplicate, or transmit any part of this document in either electronic means or in printed format. Recording of this publication is strictly prohibited and any storage of this document is not allowed unless with written permission from the publisher. All rights reserved.

The information provided herein is stated to be truthful and consistent, in that any liability, in terms of inattention or otherwise, by any usage or abuse of any policies, processes, or directions contained within is the solitary and utter responsibility of the recipient reader. Under no circumstances will any legal responsibility or blame be held against the publisher for any reparation, damages, or monetary loss due to the information herein, either directly or indirectly.

Respective authors own all copyrights not held by the publisher.

The information herein is offered for informational purposes solely, and is universal as so. The presentation of the information is without contract or any type of guarantee assurance.

The trademarks that are used are without any consent, and the publication of the trademark is without permission or backing by the trademark owner. All trademarks and brands within this book are for clarifying purposes only and are the owned by the owners themselves, not affiliated with this document.

The author is not a licensed practitioner, physician or medical professional and offers no medical treatment, diagnoses, suggestions or counseling. The information presented herein has not been evaluated by the U.S Food & Drug Administration, and it is not intended to diagnose, treat, cure or prevent any disease. Full medical clearance from a licensed physician should be obtained before beginning or modifying any diet, exercise or lifestyle program, and physician should be informed of all nutritional changes. The author claims no responsibility to any person or entity for any liability, loss or damage caused or alleged to be caused directly or indirectly as a result of the use, application or interpretation of the information presented herein.

Made in the USA
Middletown, DE
06 January 2017